# THE LONESOME THREAD

# THE LONESOME THREAD

### REFLECTIONS OF SOLITUDE, BOREDOM & CREATIVITY

## BRYAN CROSSON

NEW DEGREE PRESS

COPYRIGHT © 2020 BRYAN CROSSON

THE LONESOME THREAD

*Reflections of Solitude, Boredom & Creativity*

ISBN    978-1-63676-518-1   *Paperback*

            978-1-63676-049-0   *Kindle Ebook*

            978-1-63676-050-6   *Ebook*

LCCN:   2020477104

# CONTENTS

———

*"C'est le temps que tu as perdu pour ta rose qui fait ta rose si importante."*
—ANTOINE DE SAINT-EXUPÉRY, *LE PETIT PRINCE*

# INTRODUCTION

—

*"We have only to follow the thread of the hero path. Where we had thought to find an abomination, we shall find a god; where we had thought to slay another, we shall slay ourselves; where we had thought to travel outwards, we shall come to the center of our own existence; where we had thought to be alone, we shall be with all the world."*
—JOSEPH CAMPBELL, THE HERO WITH A THOUSAND FACES

"What a timely and important subject," my developmental editor observed over the phone when I told him I wanted to write about solitude. At the time, the world had just stepped off of the precipice and was nose-diving toward full-on pandemic, a result of the spread of the novel coronavirus, COVID-19.

To me, the importance of solitude—voluntary or otherwise—was *always* a timely subject. It is the hallmark of some of the world's greatest minds who have gifted the world with art, music, and culture. Gustav Mahler's *Wunderhorn* symphonies were composed in a stone hut completely shut off from the outside world. Jean-Michel

Basquiat was influenced by the *Gray's Anatomy* textbook he received during a month he spent in King's County Hospital recovering from an injury. Virginia Woolf advocated for women to have the space to create in solitude in her famous essay *A Room of One's Own*.

In the mid-1970s, my mother, a first-generation American of Philippine origins and the youngest of four children, walked away from her aspirations of being a brain surgeon to build a career in the performing arts. A prodigious student who graduated high school early and immediately jumped into a pre-med program, my mother quickly found that the answers she sought to life's questions did not lie in the pages of medical journals. She and my father, a talented graphic designer, have dedicated their lives to the pursuit of passion and creative endeavor.

My mother danced with ballet companies throughout the mid-Atlantic region of the United States until the mid-1980s. In 1985, her career took her to northern Italy, where she taught, performed, and choreographed all levels of classical ballet, modern dance, and jazz. There, in the mountainous Piedmont region near the Italian Alps, my parents laid the foundation upon which our family would be built. I spent my earliest years in dance studios and theaters, which privileged me with an appreciation of the arts I have carried forth into my adult life.

Deciding to chase a dream is rarely the easy choice, and it means giving up many other things the world has to offer. Living as self-described "starving artists" meant my parents experienced difficult years. Indeed, the move to Italy was in part a consequence of Reagan-era cuts in federal spending for the arts and humanities. Despite the challenges, they raised me and my brother in a way that instilled in us a different type of drive: one where the genesis of happiness comes from the pursuit of that which lies within. Central to this is the idea that discovering true interests requires introspection, imagination, and creative space.

Today, my mother is a nationally ranked competitive fencer, a sculptor, and (still) a dance teacher. Neurosurgery was not her calling—creativity was.

Some quick queries to the Internet's Oracle of Delphi (i.e., Google) reveal that social media use in the year 2020 amounted to:

- 330 million Twitter users[1]
- 706 million LinkedIn users[2]
- 1 billion Instagram users[3]
- 2.7 billion Facebook users[4]

TikTok, the politically mired video app widely considered to be the "Gen Z" medium of choice, has 800,000,000 users, 41 percent of which are between the age of sixteen

1    Ying Lin, "10 Twitter Statistics Every Marketer Should Know in 2020," *Oberlo*, May 30, 2020.

2    LinkedIn Statistics Page, accessed August 24, 2020.

3    "Instagram by the Numbers: Stats, Demographics & Fun Facts," Omnicore, accessed August 24, 2020.

4    "Number of monthly active Facebook users worldwide as of 2nd quarter 2020," Statista, accessed August 24, 2020.

and twenty-four.[5, 6] Data from media and advertising firm ZenithOptimedia predicts that the average daily time spent online on mobile devices in 2021 will top 155 minutes, a five-fold increase from a decade ago.[7] In what journalist and author Thomas Friedman describes as the "Age of Accelerations," we now are more connected than we ever have been.

Despite the amazing gifts technological advances have provided, there is growing concern that technology is changing human behaviors in ways that stifle creative freedom and critically limit the amount of time spent ideating in the present moment. Many people are beginning to rethink relationships with technology, their devices, and social media. This is not a rejection of technology, but rather a recognition of the need to make time to continue protecting and developing the most advanced piece of technology in our known existence: the human brain.

I graduated college in the wake of the Great Recession and was fortunate enough to get a jump start in life by becoming an officer in the United States Marine Corps. Despite the harsh economic conditions faced by many millennials coming of age at the time, we were clearly a generation *rich* in information. If you could afford an Internet connection, you were placed at the epoch of a revolution.

5    "Global Social Media Overview," DataReportal, accessed August 24, 2020.

6    Chris Beer. "Is TikTok Setting the Scene for Music on Social Media?" GlobalWebIndex, January 3, 2019.

7    "Daily time spent with the internet per capita worldwide from 2011 to 2021, by device," Statista, accessed August 24, 2020.

The modern world embraced the Internet as a tool and an escape. The year 2011 witnessed both the founding of Snapchat and the launch of the first "coding bootcamp" school—an escape into social media from the oft-drab present moment and a potential means of escape from an imbalanced and exorbitant system of traditional education.

I sat out of the revolution that year, largely not by choice. My time was occupied learning infantry tactics, land navigation, and combat leadership. I spent much time unplugged and disconnected from the world. Eventually, I caught up and indeed embraced the wonders of the Internet and social media. However, similar to the experience of countless service members, I spent a significant amount of time in remote, austere locales far beyond the reach of cell phone towers and Internet cafés. Probably not best to be checking Twitter while looking for improvised explosive devices in an Afghan village.

There has been a distinct ebb and flow to my interactions with both technology and my own psyche, partially due to my military career and partially because I believe carving out a distinction between the two is important. The technological habits and mindsets I formed had impacts long after I left the service. Like a foregone conclusion, I have always found myself returning to the curious and creative foundation my parents have gifted me.

The idea of unplugging is not a new one, nor is *The Lonesome Thread* an advocacy of Neo-Luddism—an outright rejection of technology. Rather, it is a collection of thoughts, reflections, and practices that can subtly change our current approach to creativity in the information age. Two of the keys to living a happier life are 1) creating time to do the "deep-down" introspection required to truly know yourself, and 2) structuring that time in a way that adds lasting value.

There is a better, healthier way to live one's inner life and to use it as a wellspring for happiness and personal endeavor. While many of the stories enclosed are reflective of my own experiences from the military, from my education, and from my life, they will hopefully inspire others to question their own status quo. Thematically, *The Lonesome Thread* is about finding or creating space, filling it with meaning rather than distraction, and using that meaning to deepen our relationships.

**HOW THIS BOOK IS STRUCTURED:**
*The Lonesome Thread* is split into three parts:

1. **Time & Space**. A collection of short stories that illuminate some of the history of solitude and withdrawal from around the world.
2. **Tools & Reflections**. Observations and best practices I have gathered that can be used to structure and fill our inner lives with intention and creativity.
3. **Creation & Gratitude**. Inspiring stories that demonstrate how periodically escaping from the world allows us to return to it in a way that gives back to those around us.

Life is best viewed from every angle possible. A true examination of a set of beliefs involves picking them up, restating them, turning them on their head, broadening or redirecting their focus, and generally kicking them around until they are a complete thought.

I will not pretend to be the first to write on the subject of inner lives, the detrimental sides of technology, or the need to periodically unplug. However, I relate these topics to my own experience walking the earth and, at the very least, will show the world from a different perspective—a prism through which introspection and creativity can be utilized in a new and enjoyable way.

The purpose of this book is not to pen a braggadocious military tell-all or another voluminous how-to guide to join special operations. Nor is it to be a "hack-your-life" self-help book. Rather, it is to illustrate the importance of comfort in solitude and the acknowledgment of the growth that occurs in the in-between moments of life. Humans are a gregarious bunch; undoubtedly it has been crucial to our survival as a species. However, every person will have a time in their life where they are alone. Solitude both in thought and in life is not something to flee from. In fact, living a healthy inner life is critical to experiencing life fully, and when we are alone is often when we do our deepest, most creative thinking. The type of thinking that then allows us to rejoin our loved ones and society as happier, more whole human beings.

# TIME & SPACE

# NAVIGATION

---

*"Vis gregis est lupus." "The strength of the pack is the wolf."*

—*MARINE SPECIAL OPERATIONS MOTTO*

Brakes squeaked over the sound of pea gravel crushing under tires as we ground to an uneven stop. A group of us had been whisked to a start point in a windowless, unmarked van. We silently exchanged glances, wondering what awaited us when the doors opened. No communication was allowed between candidates. In fact, none of us even knew the others' names. Before arriving, we had been given white engineer tape and a roll of dental floss to sew over our uniform name tapes. We used black Sharpies to carefully label our designated candidate numbers onto the tape, replacing our normal identities with rank-less, nameless digits. I was not Lieutenant Crosson. I was Candidate 017.

In early February, I was four weeks deep into the grueling selection process to become a member of the US Marine Corps' elite Special Operations unit. The previous weeks had been filled with long days of breakneck-paced runs, confidence-building (or shattering) swims, and hikes through eastern North Carolina's hinterlands. This phase of training was designed to test each candidate's knowledge of land navigation.

From the start point, everyone broke off in different directions, each man having a uniquely assigned checkpoint to which they would navigate. Candidates bounded through the tree line with quiet agility, paying barely any notice to the heavy packs they carried. Upon reaching the checkpoint and reporting to the instructor there, a new set of coordinates was provided, and the process repeated itself. The number of checkpoints each day was a mystery to all but the instructor cadre; dealing with uncertainty was part of the exercise.

Hours later, alone among the forested, rolling hills of our undisclosed training site, I exhaled a deep breath of warm air into my icy fist as I pored over my colorful topographic map. My eyes traced an invisible line from the hilltop *where I thought I was* to my next checkpoint. Distance? *Twenty-four hundred meters.* Heading? *Twenty-five degrees. North-northeast.* My knees creaked under the weight of my pack as I stood and divined a new path through the forest. No use of roads or trails was allowed.

Being fairly confident with a map and compass, I had found my first two checkpoints with relative ease. The winter sun crawled low across the mid-morning sky. I rolled a pace-count bead between my thumb and index finger. To keep track of distance traveled, many students kept a string of black beads on hand. You walk one hundred meters, you slide one bead from the top of the string down to the bottom. Once you get to ten (one thousand meters), you slide them all to the top and start over. The pace count beads were a sacred tool for navigation—and my only company deep in the woods. I shot a piercing gaze through the bare tree limbs and found my heading again, closing the distance to my checkpoint. *Eighteen hundred meters to go. Twenty-five degrees, north-northeast.* I quickly folded my map and stuffed it into my half-buttoned utility blouse for quick access. Then I was off again.

As a child, I grew up watching too many action movies. The draw to special operations was one I carried with me from some of my youngest memories through my college years and into my career in the Marine Corps. When I deployed to Afghanistan with a Marine infantry unit, I had brief opportunities to meet and work with such childhood heroes— Rangers, Green Berets, Marine Raiders, and various others from the shadows of our military's elite organizations.

Moving across the challenging wooded hillsides, I saw my past and future aligning in the present. *This is where I am supposed to be.* All of my experiences and the people I had encountered had led me to this point. I envisioned myself two years down the road, transformed into my action-movie heroes.

I rested a knee in a soft pile of leaves while I checked my map and compass again. I adjusted my pack as cold, damp sweat pressed against my body from underneath the straps. My eyes traced an invisible line on the map from my position to my next checkpoint. Twelve hundred meters to go. The compass in my other hand made my stomach drop. *I was headed in the wrong direction.*

Where had I drifted off course? How far in the wrong direction had I traveled? *Where the hell am I?*

When you are lost, a good practice is to navigate back to your last known position. Unfortunately, without knowing how far I had walked in the wrong direction, finding my way back would be nearly impossible. My special operations aspirations and action-hero dreams dissolved in front of my eyes. If I did not successfully navigate to my next point soon, it would be nearly impossible to complete the course in the (unspecified) time allotted. I frantically pulled out my map and made a futile attempt to match it to the terrain around me. With no point of reference, I might as well have been trying to navigate the dark side of the moon.

Fighting a losing battle against a deep, dark state of panic, I shot an escape azimuth on my compass. To the west was a large creek that emptied into a swamp further north. If I walked in that direction, I would not be able to miss it, and from there I could piece together my location. The only problem was I would be moving further away from my checkpoint. The sun was now hanging directly above me, diffusing its light across the drab, gray sky.

Energized with a newfound sense of urgency, I took off at a sprint. Leaping over deadfall and weaving in between trees, I closed the distance between myself and the creek, reaching its muddy banks within half an hour.

I ran north along the creekbank. Startled white-tailed deer darted in and out of my peripheral vision, trying to escape the madman who had come crashing through their thicket.

After what felt like way too damn long, the curtain of trees opened before me to reveal a misty floodplain. Standing at the intersection of the stream's terminus and the swamp, I was finally at a point I could locate on my map. I was lost no longer. I gasped in cold winter air as I gripped my compass and found a new azimuth to my checkpoint: a hilltop less than a kilometer away, directly across the swamp.

In most cases, taking the direct route over the challenging terrain is more difficult than plotting a longer route around it. This was not most cases. I did not need to look at my watch to tell that I was nearing the end of the training day. *Through the swamp it is.*

I stepped with caution, scanning the shallow wetland for emergent patches of sedge that would indicate root balls beneath to stand on. Soon I was up to my calves in wet grass and soft earth. With each step I brought myself closer to my checkpoint and deeper into the muddy water. Being soaking wet and alone in the dead of winter would present a problem, but I had already made up my mind that I would reach this checkpoint. And the next. And the next.

The hilltop came into view. I fought to free myself from densely packed vegetation just below the surface of the water. Finally reaching the shore, I scrambled up the slope. I had all but given up on reaching all my checkpoints for the day. *But I was still going to make it to this one, damn it.* The leaves and deadfall on the hillside made the thirty-meter climb feel like three hundred.

The slope leveled off. A man was seated on a campstool in a small clearing at the top of the hill. The hill had a commanding view of the entire swamp, and he no doubt had been given a front-row seat to my chilly swim. I approached the man, a khakied and bearded special operations instructor about as nondescript as a bare wall.

"Candidate zero-one-seven, ready to report," I said, deliberately enunciating each word slowly in my best attempt to compose myself and control my ragged breathing.

"Let's hear it." The instructor's bored expression told me he had probably been sitting here all day holding court for wide-eyed candidates.

I unfolded my laminated map and used a grease pen to point to my previous checkpoint.

"This is where I came from," I said, and then dragged the pen's mashed tip across miles of painful terrain to point to the hilltop in the swamp. "This is where I am."

"Okay." A reply about as ambiguous as my entire day in the woods.

It did not matter if you were the smartest, toughest, most-qualified candidate who had ever tried out for Marine Special Operations. The cadre never offered any affirmation as to whether or not you were meeting the standard. The same held true if you failed an event. An instructor would silently note your name and walk off without a word. The motivation to perform came from within each candidate, with no outside validation to indicate your standing in the course.

The instructor gave me a once-over. A mix of sweat and icy swamp water steamed off of my uniform. I mirrored his blank expression. *Give me my next checkpoint so I can get out of here.* After a long pause, he graced me with more words.

"Go sit over there," the instructor said and pointed at a copse ten meters away on the opposite side of the small hilltop. "Face away from the checkpoint, don't speak to anyone, and be prepared to move at a moment's notice."

The empty woods around me offered no sage advice. Even if I had wanted someone else to talk to, there was nobody in sight. The last part of his instruction was standard selection-speak. *Don't get comfortable here.*

As I wandered my newfound sitting area in search of a dry patch of leaves, my mind raced to figure out why I had not been given a new checkpoint. Why was I sitting here? Was I out of time? Had I failed the course? While the Marine Corps has never published the pass rate of the secretive selection course, I knew that at the end of the long battery of physical tests, leadership challenges, and psychological evaluations, most of us would indeed fail.

The overcast sky stifled the sun's glow, making it look like a dimming pearl in a sea of haze. Keeping in mind the instructions I had been given, I opened the top of my pack and changed into dry socks. I moved with a sense of urgency and a knowledge that I had to be ready *at a moment's notice.*

One boot comes off, one sock is changed, then the process is repeated on the opposite foot. That way you are never caught with two bare feet. My feet were pallid and wrinkled from the day's heavy mileage and prolonged exposure to the water. I tied my dripping wet socks into small overhand knots around the thick woven nylon straps of my pack.

Feet dry, I reclined back on my pack and tried to get as comfortable as possible as the cold began to infiltrate my damp uniform. It was as if all of my sweat had been a shadow chasing two paces behind me and, now that I had stopped, it found me in my place of rest and clung to my cold skin. Uncertainty and disappointment in my day's performance gnawed at me. *Maybe this is how selection ends for me.*

As I mulled over that thought, another candidate appeared, climbing the hill from the far side opposite the swamp. Was he late too? He reported to the instructor. Despite only being able to see their mouths moving in the distance, I knew the candidate was reciting the identical check-in script I had given a half-hour earlier. Their interaction passed equally unremarkably. The candidate nodded in response to the instructor, walked over to a spot about five meters from mine, and sat down, facing away from the checkpoint.

The sun continued to wane in the gray sky, dragging the temperature down with it. I checked my watch as a shiver coursed through my body. Being wet is one thing. Being cold is another. Being wet *and* cold is a deadly combination that can break even the hardest of spirits. I vowed that tomorrow I would make a point to pack my poncho liner at the top of my pack so I could have easy access to a shred of warmth.

Another candidate came trudging up the hill. And another. And another. Each one had a brief conversation with the instructor before taking a seat nearby. Soon, the hillside was dotted with half a dozen of us, sitting silently separated at five-meter intervals, offering blank expressions to the woods around us.

Then it dawned on me. This was my *last* scheduled checkpoint for the day. Not only had I reached every checkpoint, but I had been the first to arrive at the end point. All the self-doubt that had weighed me down throughout the day evaporated. Every instance where I had questioned my decisions and stewed in insecurity was vindicated. Despite the cold winter air, warmth and comfort filled my body. Staring off into the nothingness that hung between the darkening sky and the jagged, bare tree limbs, I reflected on my route. I watched myself struggle over hills and into draws as an impartial observer. All of the panic, dark thoughts, and hypothetical failures melted into the earth— mere impulses in my brain that brought me no closer to my objective. In the end, calm decision-making in the present moment is the only thing that gets us where we are going.

Before I had time to fully digest these thoughts, the crunch of leaves on the trail and the squeak of worn-out brakes interrupted the silence as a windowless white van climbed the hill. An almost identically indistinguishable instructor climbed out and opened the rear doors.

"Candidates," he grunted with an entirely apathetic tone. "Climb in, don't speak."

We packed ourselves into the van's cargo space, sitting on top of our rucksacks to make enough room. The doors slammed shut, bathing us in darkness, and the wheels began to turn. No more land navigation for us today. We would have many more miles of silent walking tomorrow, and the next day, and in the weeks to come, but with each day we were filled with new confidence in ourselves and our abilities.

At the end of the course, to my great relief, I was selected. In retrospect, the key to passing is unwavering resolution— knowing who you are and what exactly you are all about. For this reason, navigating through the woods alone with confidence is one of the most essential skills during special operations selection. In a similar vein, we must learn to navigate ourselves before we can confidently live our best life among others. Making decisions alone in an uncertain world with no feedback as to whether you are on the right path feels unnatural at first. However, making a practiced habit of it is like discovering an innate superpower. Life is an ambiguous journey in which the only true certainties lie within each individual. We too often struggle to understand others before even making a single attempt to understand ourselves. The world is built on collaboration, but when building yourself, the first and most important counsel you should keep is your own.

# RETREAT

—

*"In order to understand the world, one has to turn away from it on occasion; in order to serve men better, one has to hold them at a distance for a time."*

—ALBERT CAMUS, THE MINOTAUR

Armies retreat from battle; executives go on corporate retreats. Retreat signifies a withdrawal to a different place. But what is it that makes the idea of retreat so valuable and powerful?

For Andy Puddicombe, the bald-headed Buddhist-monk-turned-cofounder of the popular meditation app Headspace, spending a decade in retreat in the snow-capped Himalayas was the only way to change the direction he saw his life headed.

Born in London in 1972, Andy grew up in the small parish of Keynsham, located at the confluence of the River Chew and River Avon, halfway between Bristol and Bath. A location of prehistoric island tribes, the area was first conquered by the Romans at the start of the first millennium, and later by William the Conqueror in the Middle Ages. A census ordered by King William identified Keynsham as a "hundred" in the county of Somerset with a total population of 209.[8] It became a chartered market town around 1170, when the Keynsham Abbey was founded. In the twentieth century, the Cadbury chocolate factory became the town's most prominent employer.

Growing up in the 1970s, Andy's childhood was anything but normal. In a sleepy town full of blue-collar tradespeople, his mother, a psychotherapist and acupuncturist, broke the mold. She raised him in a progressive household, where alternative medicine replaced doctor visits, yogurt cultures grew in the kitchen, and they had a sensory deprivation tank in the garage.

When he was eleven, Andy's parents divorced. Andy's mother took a weekly meditation class to deal with the stress, to which he and his sister often accompanied her. While he enjoyed the experience, he knew most teens in the mid '80s were not spending their Monday nights sitting cross-legged on a carpeted studio floor. Despite the New Age flavor of his upbringing, Andy was still a kid growing up in England and, like many boys of his age, much of his spare time was spent out on the pitch playing rugby or football.

At age sixteen he "discovered girls, beer, and nights out."[9] He attended De Montfort University in Leicester where he

---

8   A hundred is defined by Oxford Languages as "a subdivision of a county or shire, having its own court." Keynsham's population as recorded in the Domesday Book included villagers, smallholders, slaves, "other population," and burgesses. Anna Powell-Smith, "Keynsham," Open Domesday, accessed October 7, 2020.

9   P Funk, "Declutter your mind on the Central Line," *Evening Standard*, April 14, 2010.

studied sports science. There, along the banks of the River Soar, his days were occupied with football, rugby, and tennis and his nights were spent in pubs on High Street chasing girls.

One Christmas Eve, as Andy, home for the holidays, stepped out of a disco at the Keynsham Rugby Club with his friends, his life trajectory was forever altered in an instant. Standing among a crowd in the taxi queue outside of the club in the cold night, he narrowly avoided a car careening down Bristol Road and watched helplessly as it jumped the curb and plowed into the group behind him. "There were bodies flying everywhere," Andy recalled in a 2010 interview with the *Evening Standard*, "almost like something out of a movie… It was horrific."[10]

The crash killed a twenty-one-year-old mother and a local rugby player and left another eight in critical condition.[11] "It had a major impact on my life," he described. "It made me question what I was doing and why. It forced me to look at the fragility of life. But most of all, it gave me an insight into how difficult and painful life can be sometimes, and how we all need a way of coping with this stuff, no matter how big or small."[12]

Andy returned to De Montfort, but the trauma left him with a restless dissatisfaction with life. "No matter how much beer I drank or how many women I slept with or what my grades were—nothing hit the spot."[13]

---

10  Ibid.
11  David Connett, "Second victim in Christmas crash," *The Independent*, December 27, 1992.
12  P Funk, "Declutter your mind on the Central Line."
13  Ibid.

Three months later, Andy's twenty-year-old stepsister was struck by a vehicle while riding her bicycle. Not long after, an ex-girlfriend with whom he was close friends with died during heart surgery. It was almost too much to handle. Andy traveled to put distance between himself and the tragedies, but heavy thoughts of his friends still weighed on his mind. Returning to school did not help. Andy wrestled with the feeling that life had more to offer than chasing an education and career with which he was becoming increasingly dispassionate.

Sitting in his dorm room after a class, Andy experienced a breakthrough. In the afternoon quietude, a feeling swept over him that he could only describe as "deeply moving."[14] It lasted for several hours, and when it passed, the message was clear: Twenty-two-year-old Andy Puddicombe would become a Buddhist monk. Energized, he walked across campus and quit university that afternoon.

Lisa Directo-Davis, program director at the John Main Center for Meditation and Inter-religious Dialogue at Georgetown University, calls life-shaping experiences such as Andy's "catalysts." Life is full of catalysts that are in some way a key to a deeper being, an anthropology of self. She explains, "Being human is transcendent—it has the capacity to transform and grow." Lisa does not believe these experiences transform us into new people—rather, they give us "a remembering of ourselves as our truest self."

---

14  Lizzie Widdicombe, "The Higher Life," *The New Yorker,* June 29, 2015.

These catalysts drove Andy to Northern India, pursuing the deeper meaning he knew was out there. The transformation began from the moment he first crossed the threshold into a monastery. As the monastery's barber sheared Andy's head bald for the first time, there was an emotional unburdening. The act of renunciation requires giving up not only worldly belongings but worldly identity, and the old Andy Puddicombe began to fade into the background. He spent a short stint as a novice monk in the Tibetan tradition, a practice overwhelmingly rich with complex history and culture. Eventually, Andy migrated to Myanmar and spent five years at a school practicing in the Burmese Theravāda tradition.

Buddhism originated in India around the fifth century BCE. It was founded on principles laid out by "the Buddha" and centers on overcoming suffering by achieving enlightenment (i.e., Nirvana). Mindfulness and meditation are common practices in Buddhist traditions.

Theravāda Buddhism, literally translated to "School of the Elders," is the oldest, most traditional Buddhist practice. The focus of Theravāda Buddhism is attaining self-liberation through individual efforts. Theravāda practitioners must use the Buddha's original teachings to create their own path to enlightenment without the help of deities. Consequently, meditation and concentration are important practices to attaining nirvana and true insight into the nature of reality. Full-time monastic life is a hallmark of this tradition.

In Tibet, Buddhism was introduced in the eighth century CE at the request of Trisong Detsen, the country's thirty-eighth emperor. Tibetan Buddhism combined the Mahayana Buddhist philosophies with Tantric practices such as deity yoga and material from a native Tibetan religion called Bon. Tibetan Buddhism has a strong emphasis on outwardly religious activities and deeply symbolic ritual practices rather than the inner spiritual life.

For practicing Buddhist monks, most time is spent in retreat. Andy's first days practicing were filled with excitement about this new way of life. However, once the honeymoon period wore off, the reality began to set in. This was a place for introspection, not relaxation. Andy, the athlete and sports science student from England, discovered he had to accustom his body to handle a completely different kind of rigor.

"I was so used to expending that energy and now I was just sitting there with my eyes closed," Andy described in a podcast for WHOOP, a fitness and lifestyle biometrics company.[15] It was taxing in brand new ways. Andy's knees ached from hours sitting in lotus. When not in retreat, four to eight hours of Andy's day were spent in meditation. However, during periods of retreat, meditation occupied the entire day. "People have a rather romantic view of monastic life," Andy observed. "The idea of a month away from all the hassles in life sounds appealing. But then what? The one and only thing you have to look at is yourself."[16]

Andy jumped in headfirst, spending a month in retreat and meditating morning to evening, between seventeen to eighteen hours per day, alternating between walking and sitting. Monks in retreat only sleep three to four hours a day and every waking moment is spent in utter silence. As time passed, he began to experience a calm that he had never experienced in his nearly thirty years of life. His next stint in retreat lasted three months.

---

15    Will Ahmed, "Andy Puddicombe, Buddhist Monk and Co-Founder of Headspace," 27 February 2019, In *WHOOP Podcast*, Podcast, MP3 audio, 1:29:22.

16    P Funk, "Declutter your mind on the Central Line."

Theravāda is also the most conservative of Buddhism traditions. The strict adherence to the Buddha's original teachings and disciplined rules of monastic life eventually began to take a toll on Andy. Locked behind the walls of a monastery and isolated for months at a time, he began to miss his friends and family. The pot finally boiled over, resulting in Andy mounting a midnight escape. Under the cover of darkness, he snuck out to the garden, climbed a sturdy pine tree, and disappeared over the monastery walls.[17]

Andy remained in South Asia, returning to the Tibetan tradition of Buddhism, in which he eventually became a fully ordained monk. After spending a full year isolated from the world in retreat, he relocated to Russia and spent the next four years continuing his studies while teaching meditation. Thrust back into civilization, he began to reacclimate himself to the world, rebuilding his muscle strength after years without any regular fitness routine, and with a friend attended a circus school run by the Moscow State Circus.

In Moscow, the post-USSR economic boom meant a wide range of businessmen, travelers, and expats from around the world visited the meditation center at which Andy worked. BP had just established its Russian joint venture, TNK-BP, as a result of the merger of Russian companies TNK, Sidanko, and Onako with the majority of BP's Russian oil assets.[18] A senior executive asked Andy to visit their local office to

17  Andy Puddicombe, *The Headspace Guide to Meditation and Mindfulness: How Mindfulness Can Change Your Life in Ten Minutes a Day*, (New York: St. Martin's Publishing Group, 2012), 1.

18  "BP in Russia: a timeline," *The Guardian*, October 18, 2012, accessed August 24, 2020.

provide some guided meditation for his team but was wary of how Andy's maroon monk robes might look in the midst of a conference room full of Savile Row suits. "You know what?" he said. "Coming in dressed like that to an oil company in Russia, it's just never going to work."[19] Andy quickly realized that while demand for meditation was growing at a rapid pace, his monk attire might be distracting. "Not everyone was comfortable with the 'bald-headed-guy-in-a-skirt' thing. I couldn't help thinking that there must be an accessible way."[20]

With six months left on his Russian religious "monk" visa, Andy began to think about the future. He had nothing, having renounced the possessions of his previous life—clothing and money included—when he had first come to Asia. In a moment of serendipity, Andy realized that he could use his training with the Moscow State Circus to return to England, which at the time offered generous grants and funding for students.[21]

Andy returned to London in 2004. He studied circus arts and acrobatics at the Conservatoire of Dance and Drama by day while continuing his practice as a holistic doctor teaching mindfulness and meditation by night. At thirty-two, Andy was significantly older than the students around him and such an outlier that the Conservatoire had him sign a release of liability in the event that he injured himself.[22] Andy also

19  "Get Some Headspace: Q&A with Andy Puddicombe," Beach Tomato, accessed August 24, 2020.

20  P Funk, "Declutter your mind on the Central Line."

21  Rachel Jacqueline, "Headspace app co-founder and monk Andy Puddicombe talks mindfulness," *Post Magazine*, May 30, 2015.

22  Will Ahmed, "Andy Puddicombe, Buddhist Monk and Co-Founder of Headspace."

became more involved in the greater movement to incorporate meditation into mainstream healthcare, and he became
registered as a clinical meditation consultant with the UK
Healthcare Commission. It was through his meditation practice that he met Richard Pierson.

In 2008, twenty-seven-year-old Londoner Rich Pierson was
a burnt-out marketing executive working for a major agency
representing Axe body spray.[23] Finally reaching a breaking
point, he left his firm and began looking for the next thing,
freelancing to keep himself afloat. Despite his newfound
freedom, he was wracked with anxiety, struggling to even
go out in public. Pierson turned to meditation as a means
of coping.[24]

Andy and Pierson were connected by a mutual friend. The
two bonded over a relatable experience of trying to explain
the concept of mindfulness to people. Pierson's only prior
experience meditating was a brief and unsuccessful teen-
age experience similar to Puddicombe's early attempts. He
immediately recognized the genius of Andy's approach. "This
is a guy who went and sat on his backside eighteen hours
a day for ten years. If you're using the ten-thousand-hour
thing, he's done that and more," Pierson explained in a *Fast
Company* interview. "He's so good at explaining it, and it's
not weird."[25]

---

23  Lauren Goode, and Kara Swisher, "Headspace meditation app co-founder
    and CEO Rich Pierson," July 7, 2017, In Too Embarrassed to Ask,
    produced by Vox Media, Podcast, MP3 audio, 47:08.
24  Kathleen Chaykowski, "Meet Headspace, The App That Made Meditation
    A $250 Million Business," *Forbes*, January 8, 2017.
25  Bill Barol, "The Monk And The Mad Man Making Mindfulness For The
    Masses," *Fast Company*, January 28, 2015.

Business-savvy Pierson recognized an opportunity to reach millions around the world through a meditation app. Pierson pitched Andy the idea of "creating the Nike+ of meditation."[26] Andy and Pierson partnered, founding their company, Headspace, with the mission "to get as many people in the world as possible to take ten minutes out of their day, to practice a simple and easy-to-learn meditation technique and experience the scientifically proven benefits of meditation."[27]

Andy was initially uncertain about the idea of an app. He had been writing content for years, but most of it up to this point had largely been turned into manuals for corporate work and to train people to teach meditation. The concept of an app was still brand new to the world. When Andy had left for Asia almost twenty years prior, the idea of a smartphone was inconceivable. In a 2015 interview published in *Post Magazine*, Andy described the dilemma. "I didn't know what the internet was completely; I didn't have email or a mobile phone. I only got a Facebook account six months ago."[28]

The pair began by writing and selling a book, *Get Some Headspace*, running workshops to raise money, talking about the benefits of meditation, and leading group meditation sessions. By spring 2010, through the book advance and loans from friends and family, Pierson and Andy had raised $50,000, which they used to launch Headspace as an events company

---

26  Will Ahmed, "Andy Puddicombe, Buddhist Monk and Co-Founder of Headspace."

27  Andy Puddicombe, "Why 10 Minutes Each Day Can Change Your Day," Produced by DO Wales, *DO*. 2012, Video, 20:17.

28  Rachel Jacqueline, "Headspace app co-founder and monk Andy Puddicombe talks mindfulness."

offering ten-week guided meditation courses, which Andy led. They poured their profits into the development of the first version of the Headspace app—a set of 365 meditation sessions narrated by Andy.[29] The app's cartoonish animations reflected Andy's background in circus performing and gave meditation an approachable and entertaining flavor. Tiny colorful figures juggled balls and danced across phone screens around the world as Headspace began to rack up downloads. For Rich and Andy, it was a make-or-break moment.

"We were very lucky," Andy told *Post Magazine*. "*The Guardian* newspaper picked up what we were doing and paid for one million booklets to go in the newspaper advertising the app. That really got us started."[30] Headspace was a bona fide start-up.

Since then, Headspace has grown to enormous proportions. In 2015, Rich and Andy closed a $30 million Series A round of fundraising, led by entertainment-focused investment firm The Chernin Group. Also included in the Series A were investors such as Jessica Alba, Jared Leto, Ryan Seacrest, and LinkedIn Chief Executive Jeff Weiner, a longtime proponent of mindfulness practices and meditation.[31]

In 2017, Headspace's annual revenue was north of $50 million, with a valuation estimated by *Forbes* to be roughly $250 million.[32] The app is now used by over sixty million people

29  Kathleen Chaykowski, "Meet Headspace, The App That Made Meditation A $250 Million Business."

30  Rachel Jacqueline, "Headspace app co-founder and monk Andy Puddicombe talks mindfulness."

31  Kathleen Chaykowski, "Meet Headspace, The App That Made Meditation A $250 Million Business."

32  Ibid.

worldwide.[33] Andy, still an avid sports fan, works with organizations ranging from the NBA to Arsenal Football Club to improve athletic performance through mindfulness. Headspace is also currently working on seventy clinical studies supported by academic partners such as Carnegie Mellon, the University of California, San Francisco, and Stanford University.[34]

Andy's withdrawal from society created the space he needed to change his mindset and thus his life's trajectory. His disciplined adherence to mindfulness and meditation practices helped him in 2013 when he was diagnosed with testicular cancer. While he expected the physical pain of undergoing surgery to remove his right testicle, he was surprised by the emotional and mental impact it had on him. "Mindfulness was, has been, and continues to be integral to my recovery," he explained in an interview with *Thrive Global*.[35]

Headspace's chief medical officer Dr. David Cox now recommends cancer patients at least ten to forty minutes of mindfulness practice a day.[36] Headspace even has thirty sessions available uniquely dedicated to "Coping with Cancer."

---

33  David Silverberg, "Scaling mindfulness: How the Headspace cofounders used the NBA, Delta Airlines, and The Guardian newspaper to bring meditation to 60 million users," *Business Insider*, November 29, 2019.

34  Jonathan Shieber, "Headspace raises $93 Million in equity and debt as it pursues clinical validation for mindfulness," *Tech Crunch*, February 12, 2020.

35  Sunita Sehmi, "Meditation isn't about eliminating stress from your life it's about learning to sit with it. Andy Puddicombe invites us all to get some Headspace," *Thrive Global*, May 20, 2019.

36  Matthew Jenkin, "Mind over cancer: can meditation aid recovery?" *The Guardian*, February 14, 2020.

The tragedy Andy experienced early on in life served as the catalyst that drove him to seek out a greater purpose. However, it is important to note that much of Andy's path needed to be walked alone. "Retreat combines solitude and the practice of meditation, where you begin to actually explore your own mind," Buddhist scholar Reggie Ray, who leads meditation retreats at Shambhala Mountain Center in Red Feather Lakes, Colorado, explained for *Tricycle* magazine. "What you find is that, through intensive meditation in retreat, you begin to attend to your mind in a direct and unmediated way: Your mind begins to slow down, your sense perceptions open up, you find yourself increasingly present to your life, and you begin to experience solitude in a deep and genuine way."[37]

Only by first navigating that path of solitude was Andy able to rejoin the rest of the world and go on to positively impact millions of lives around the world. This is not a call to action encouraging people to abandon city life and flock into the hills of Northern India and take a Buddhist monk's vow of silence. Rather, this is a case for seeking out an inner silence among the bustle of modern life. Indeed, Albert Camus writes in *The Myth of Sisyphus*: "Silence is no longer possible except in noisy cities. From Amsterdam Descartes writes to the aged Guez de Balzac: 'I go out walking every day amid the confusion of a great crowd, with as much freedom and tranquility as you could do on your garden paths.'"[38]

Where do we find the "great crowds" in our daily lives? They do not exist solely in the physical world. Just like how taking

---

37  Ted Rose, "The Power of Solitude," *Tricycle*, Spring 2005.

38  Albert Camus, *The Myth of Sisyphus and Other Essays*, Translated by Justin O'Brien, (New York: Random House LLC, 2012), 100.

a trip out to the countryside for a change of scenery can provide a sense of relief and escape, so should the mind occasionally seek refuge from constant overcrowding. In many of his meditations, Andy uses the metaphor of the mind as a clear blue sky—a blank canvas. Our thoughts are like clouds passing by, and even though at times we cannot see anything but storm clouds overhead, the blue sky is still there, far above them.

Endless to-do lists, meetings, happy hours, social outings, and all of the other potpourri that persistently call for our attention have a way of crowding the sky above us. Taking a few moments to clear our mind can provide needed perspective so we do not get overwhelmed in life's frenetic pace. With a wealth of modern resources available—many for free—we have no reason not to try on a monk's (metaphoric) robes for ten minutes. All the demands of life will remain when you close your eyes, but when you open them again, for a fleeting moment in time, you can sit still, breathe out, and enjoy a piece of blue sky.

# RETROGRADE

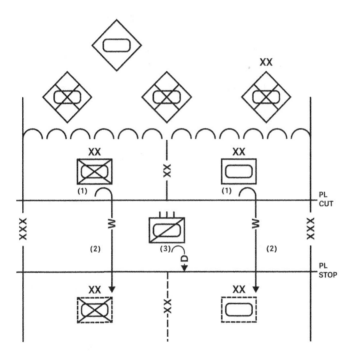

A graphic depiction of a military withdrawal. The diamonds represent enemy units while the rectangles represent friendly forces.

*Retrograde: "A defensive task that involves organized move-*
*ment away from the enemy. The enemy may force these oper-*
*ations, or a commander may execute them voluntarily... The*
*retrograde is a transitional operation; it is not conducted in*
*isolation. It is part of a larger scheme of maneuver designed*
*to regain the initiative and defeat the enemy."*

—ARMY DOCTRINE REFERENCE PUBLICATION

(ADRP) 3-90, OFFENSE AND DEFENSE

Almost thirty-eight degrees north of the Earth's equatorial
plane (i.e., the equator) you can find Headspace's San Francisco headquarters on California Street, the long thorough-
fare that connects the Financial District with the oceanside
mansions of Frisco's opulent Sea Cliff neighborhood. If you
were to continue traveling west along that latitude across
the Pacific Ocean (a quick, 5,800-mile trip), you would find
yourself standing in the middle of the Korean peninsula's
infamous Demilitarized Zone. Standing in stark contrast
to Andy Puddicombe's solitary retreat into the mountains
of India, the Korean peninsula is the site of one of the
largest military evacuations in history. However, much
like Andy's story, this withdrawal was the only choice to
prevent disaster.

Field Manual 100-15 is the guiding document for how to use
the US Army corps to conduct major military operations. A
"corps" is the largest tactical unit in a military's arsenal, and
usually made up of between fifty thousand and one hundred
thousand troops. While infantry (i.e., trigger-pullers) make
up the majority of the force, troops come from a wide variety
of jobs ranging from artillery to support (e.g., communications, medicine, logistics, etc.). A corps' strength lies in its

flexibility and scalability—its ability to organize multiple units from all around the US military under its command.

The term's origin comes from the Napoleonic wars, where Napoleon split his Grande Armée into smaller, more agile armies capable of working independently without relying on support from one another. These Corps d'Armée gave Napoleon a distinct advantage over his opponents and allowed him to (briefly) dominate the European continent.

In late 1950, the US Army's X Corps, part of the United Nations mission to assist South Korea after a massive North Korean invasion, had single-handedly turned the tide of the war through an audacious surprise landing at the port city of Inchon, seventeen miles west of Seoul. Comprised of US Army, US Marine Corps, and Republic of Korea (ROK) forces, X Corps attacked up the Korean peninsula toward the Yalu River, on the border between North Korea and China.

With the North Korean army scattered and on the run, General Douglas MacArthur, the commander of the UN force, announced, "You tell the boys that when they get to the Yalu (River) they are going home. I want to make good on my statement that they are going to eat Christmas dinner at home."[39]

Unbeknownst to MacArthur, Chinese leader Mao Zedong had ordered the People's Volunteer Army to infiltrate over the border and prepare a counterattack. Intelligence reports

---

39   "Home by Christmas" by General Douglas MacArthur, November 28, 1950.

began indicating that Chinese forces had crossed the Yalu River and entered North Korea. However, they estimated the People's Volunteer Army strength to be seventy thousand—half the size of the UN coalition.

On the night of November 27, the People's Volunteer Army launched a massive surprise attack on the advancing UN forces. Three hundred thousand Chinese soldiers ambushed US and ROK forces, moving quickly in an effort to cut off any attempts at retreat.

One element of X Corps, the 1st Marine Division out of Camp Pendleton, CA, found itself on the ropes against the People's Volunteer Army, battling it out around a snowy man-made lake named Changjin Reservoir, better known to the UN Forces as the Chosin Reservoir—its name on the old Japanese maps they had been issued. The twenty-five thousand Marines, strung out along several miles of the reservoir's western side, were swarmed by Chinese assaulters.

"You didn't have to look where they were," John "Red" Parkinson, a US Marine with the 1st Marine Division's 7th Marines Regiment, described the situation in a PBS interview for the *American Experience* documentary *The Battle of Chosin*. "In back of ya, in front of ya, around ya... right in the middle of ya."[40] The first morning of the attack was John's twenty-second birthday.

---

40  *American Experience*, season 28, episode 8, "The Battle of Chosin," directed by Randall MacLowry, aired November 1, 2016, on PBS.

John and ninety-five other Marines defended a portion of road near the village of Yudam-ni. Their job was to prevent Chinese mechanized forces from advancing south and destroying the rest of the regiment. His squad leader and best friend, Sergeant Robert Devins, was shot in the head. "Bob got killed," Parkinson recalled, "and died in my and my buddy's arms. We put him in a sleeping bag and laid him by the road, knowing graves registration would pick him up." Parkinson was devastated, but the fighting continued. "There were ninety-six of us on that road, and six came out."[41]

"You'd be shooting, you'd be stabbing, using your rifle as a club," Bob Boulden, a Marine rifleman with the 1st Signal Battalion, recalled for PBS. "Sometimes they'd be six, eight feet away from you, before you even knew it, and that's when either you bayonet or your rifle becomes a club."[42]

Days of constant combat blended together. Much of the fighting occurred on the mountainous Kaema Plateau in the North Korean highland. A cold front out of Siberia had blown down over the region, plummeting temperatures to an estimated –35° Fahrenheit, freezing the roads, vehicles, and weapons.[43]

There on the frigid "roof of Korea," the climate was as deadly as the enemy. Snow piled as high as men's waists. "Thirty-five below zero seems to be the agreed-upon low," Private First

---

41  Mary Lou Walters, "Hero Of The Chosin Reservoir," *The Eastwick Press*, April 11, 2014.

42  *American Experience*, season 28, episode 8, "The Battle of Chosin."

43  Roy Appleman, *Escaping the Trap: The US Army X Corps in Northeast Korea, 1950*, (College Station, Texas: Texas A&M University), 1990.

Class Jim Evans, an infantryman assigned to 1st Marine Regiment, recalled years later for a Legacy Washington profile. "That's not counting the wind chill, so when some guys say it was 50 below maybe that's their rationale. When it gets that cold, another 10 degrees doesn't matter much. I couldn't feel my feet unless I stomped up and down and kept moving. But I kept them dry. That was important. Some guys lost their toes. Others their feet."[44]

Both sides sustained massive losses as the cold temperatures froze radio batteries, medical supplies, and even gun lubricants, causing combat to devolve into bloody close-range engagements along the ridges surrounding the reservoir. The ground was too frozen to dig foxholes, causing troops to resort to piling frozen bodies for cover.[45]

Medics warmed morphine syrettes in their mouths to thaw them enough to be administered.[46] Combatants walked around with frozen bullet wounds, not discovering them until they reached the warmth of a tent and died of blood loss.[47] John Parkinson, still in the fight, helped evacuate the wounded to the rear. After dropping a Marine off at an aid station, he lingered in the warmth of the tent, basking in a moment of respite from the horror outside. Having lost a glove during the fighting, John stood with his right hand jammed into his field jacket. All around him the wounded

---

44   John C. Hughes, *Jim Evans*, (Olympia, Washington: Legacy Washington), 2017, 2.

45   Volker Janssen, "The Most Harrowing Battle of the Korean War," History, accessed August 25, 2020.

46   John C. Hughes, *Jim Evans*. 15.

47   Volker Janssen, "The Most Harrowing Battle of the Korean War."

lay on straw mats in the makeshift hospital. One wounded man noticed John standing there and asked him if he was headed back out to fight. John said yes.

"Then take this." The wounded Marine offered his own glove. "I won't need it anymore."

As John reached for the glove, he noticed the Marine was missing his right arm.[48]

The Chinese forces had the entire 1st Marine Division surrounded. As the situation around the Chosin Reservoir grew more dire, MacArthur and his generals decided that the Marines had no choice but to withdraw their forces out of the area.

You will rarely hear military planners utter the word "retreat." The reason is that the term simply does not exist in any US military doctrine. Instead, Field Manual 100-15 defines "withdrawal," one of several types of retrograde movements, as "a planned operation in which a force in contact disengages from an enemy force." Some reasons given for a withdrawal are:

- To move away from the enemy to reposition forces on more favorable terrain.
- To conserve resources for future operations.
- To gain time.
- To avoid combat under unfavorable conditions.[49]

---

48   Mary Lou Walters, "Hero Of The Chosin Reservoir."
49   *Field Manual 100-15: Corps Operations*, (Washington, DC: Department of the Army, 1996), 202.

Much like Andy Puddicombe's withdrawal from society was a necessary change in direction, so is a military withdrawal. The 1st Marine Division was at risk of total annihilation in what became known as the "Frozen Chosin." General Oliver P. Smith, the commander of 1st Marine Division, famously proclaimed, "Retreat, hell. We're not retreating. We're just advancing in another direction."[50]

THE ROAD BACK – Astonished Marines of the 5th and 7th Regiments, who hurled back a surprise onslaught by three Chinese communist divisions hear that they are to withdraw! In five days and nights of below zero winds and icy roads, from November 28 to December 3, they fought back fifteen miles through Chinese hordes to Hagaru-ri on the southern tip of Chosin Reservoir, where they are organized for the epic forty-mile fight down mountain trails to the sea. They brought out their wounded and their equipment. 1stMarDiv. Yudam-ni. By: Sgt. F. C. Kerr.

---

50   Volker Janssen, "The Most Harrowing Battle of the Korean War."

Vicious fighting centered around a seventy-eight-mile stretch of road that led south to safety. Over seventeen days, Marines fought tooth-and-nail to dislodge Chinese forces from the icy peaks and mountain passes overlooking the road. Combat raged day and night, with the People's Volunteer Army defending their positions to the last man. Marines captured positions only to find that enemy fighters had frozen overnight in their foxholes.[51]

Finally, at 9 p.m. on December 11, the last of the weary Marines and UN forces reached the friendly-held North Korean port of Hungnam, where friendly ships awaited to embark them. On Christmas Eve, the last UN forces were evacuated from Hungnam. What remained of X Corp was redeployed to the south to support US forces still engaged in heavy combat around the thirty-eighth parallel.[52]

The Chinese and North Korean forces fought the UN to a stalemate, and armistice negotiations began in July of 1951, eventually resulting in the Korean Armistice Agreement of 1953. General Smith was credited with saving the UN Forces at Chosin from complete destruction by commanding the retreat to Hungnam. The Marine Corps University, the professional military education institute located in Quantico Virginia, uses Smith's actions in Korea as a case study on resilience. His "advance in another direction" mantra strengthened the psychological armor of his trapped Marines. "By maintaining an offensive mindset (attacking or preparing

51    Alexander Bevin, *Korea: The First War We Lost*, (New York: Hippocrene Books, 1986), 364.

52    Billy C. Mossman, *Ebb and Flow: November 1950-July 1951*, (Washington, DC: U.S. Government Printing Office, 1990), 157-160.

to attack), [Smith] built resolve throughout the Division." The case study asserts that Smith's "leadership provided a level of resiliency to his Marines that carried forward throughout their lives."[53]

Withdrawal in both battle and in life is often necessitated by a situation that is unfavorable or unsustainable. In the context of substance and drug abuse, withdrawal symptoms can be the source of excruciating pain and anxiety. In every meaning of the word, it is the ability to regain homeostasis, the equilibrium required for normal functioning life. Withdrawal is uncomfortable, for in many cases it is an admission that we have walked the wrong path; however, it is something we do or go through at a time when the only alternative is destruction.

For Andy, withdrawal meant leaving school—and the rest of the world—*for a decade.* It prevented him from traveling down what he saw was a dead-end path and eventually allowed him to return to society and help millions of people.

In our modern life, the concept of a retreat as means of maintaining personal wellness and mental health has taken off. Data from the Global Wellness Institute estimates that wellness tourism was a $639 billion market in 2017, projected to grow to over $900 billion by 2022. Corporate wellness programs are a sought-after employee benefit, especially as views on work-life balance evolve. At the peak of the 2020 coronavirus pandemic, Headspace saw up to a 90 percent

---

53  *Commandership at the Chosin Reservoir: A Triumph of Optimism and Resilience,* (Quantico, VA: Marine Corps University, 2019), 56-57.

increase in time spent on mobile devices in the US week after week.[54]

Most importantly, the concept of wellness is often never the focus of conversation until things in life are not well. In many cases, only when we are dangled over the precipice do we realize we have not done the serious inner work to come to terms with the fact that we need to change direction, even if only for a moment of respite.

Andy Puddicombe retreated to the most remote parts of the world, but eventually rejoined society a stronger and wiser human being. Military withdrawals are conducted as a means to avoid operations in unfavorable conditions, yet that does not mean they are considered defeats. Do not look at the concept of retreat as an admission of failure. Rather, look at it as a way to advance in another direction.

So, what happens when there is nowhere to go?

54  Elad Natanson, "Healthcare Apps: A Boon, Today And Tomorrow," *Forbes*, July 21, 2020.

# ISOLATION

---

*"Immediately prescribe some character and form of conduce
to yourself, which you may keep both alone and in company."*
—EPICTETUS, THE ENCHIRIDION, 135 ACE

Darkness. Nothing around me but darkness. Time has lost all
meaning at this point—they took my watch. A fatigue seeps
down from my skin and wraps itself around my bones. My
brain sends signals down to the rest of my body, sweeping
from head to toe, checking to make sure it's all still there.

As my eyes adjust to the darkness, I take stock of my surroundings. I stretch my arms halfway out and touch the cold,
rough concrete on either side of me. By a quick estimate, my
cinderblock cell is three by three and a half feet—intentionally just small enough to keep me from fully stretching out
or lying down. A single cinderblock is cemented to the wall
opposite the cell's large metal door, the only place to sit. Next
to this "chair" is a large tin can, which now is a toilet.

Sound begins to creep in. A grainy, haunting recording of
Rudyard Kipling's poem "Boots" drones on from a speaker

just outside. The tempo and volume begin at a whisper, but eventually increase to a fever pitch, the speaker screaming, mainlining the insanity of life in the colonial infantry directly into my brain. The repetitive verses finally reach a summit, as the speaker blares, "AN' THERE'S NO DISCHARGE IN THE WAR."

There is a moment of respite from the racket, then static scratching over the speaker, a needle drop onto vinyl, and the poem starts from the beginning: "We're foot... slog... slog... slog... sloggin' over Africa...."

My fingers sting from the cold. I rub my hands together and warm them up until I have just enough dexterity to fish out the dog tag wedged into my boot. Adjusting my body in the confining space of the cell, I use it to carve my initials into the side of the wall as proof of life and identity for rescuers who will never arrive. I go back to squatting on my cinderblock chair and stare at the door. My gaze burns a hole through it and into another dimension, where my mind floats untethered.

I blink myself back into the present. Frozen sweat cracks around the corners of my eyes. I remind myself of who I am: a student (once again). This is survival school. I am trapped like a wild animal—captured. Held prisoner immersed in this educational experience.

Outside of these new accommodations are long passageways that snake throughout the "prison." Identical cells line the walls, jam-packing students throughout the facility. Up until this point we had been living in the woods, honing our skills in the outdoors. We learned to subsist on a diet of whatever the forest provided: small game, wild onions and potatoes, even some mussels we had pulled from a swamp and steamed on the blade of an entrenching tool over a fire.

Over the past week we had been pursued relentlessly by SERE (short for Survival, Evasion, Resistance, and Escape, pronounced "sear") instructors. To escape them, we walked endlessly—concealing our footprints behind us, crossing streams in an effort to throw off the Belgian Malinois dogs used to track us, and only resting deep inside brambles where not even the local fauna dared to venture.

The thing to know about SERE school is that everybody gets captured eventually. At that point, the "Survival, Evasion" portion of the training ends, and the "Resistance, Escape" portion begins. We traded our thorny forest hideouts for these concrete cells. With no windows or clocks, days and nights blend together into a gray mental haze.

Psychological propaganda blares over the prison's speaker system at all hours. The only break from the omnipresent cacophony is when my cell door swings open, a bag is thrown over my head, and I am whisked away to another room for interrogation.

The interrogations vary in terms of method and approach, but all are designed to break the human psyche. I resist and resist and resist, until I can resist no more—at which point the interrogation ends, the bag goes back over the head, and I am led back to my cell where I bathe in solitude.

Alone in my thoughts, I ignore the temptation to dive down a rabbit hole of despair. Bereft of any contact, maintaining emotional and psychological composure is a challenge every student faces. The silent learning imparted in a lonely training cell becomes more valuable than the PowerPoint lessons that had been beamed onto the wall of a tidy classroom what felt like a lifetime ago (just two weeks ago, as it turns out).

SERE school was first created by the US Air Force in its nascent days following World War II. Eventually, all branches of the military created some version of the training, focusing on preparing personnel for deployment to high risk areas around the world. Today, military personnel assigned to units whose missions involve a high risk of capture are sent through SERE. Much of the curriculum remains classified, but the value of the training is obvious—SERE school unlocks a set of tools for the worst-case scenarios of war. Ideally, most graduates never need to reach into their toolkit and use the tools, *but they are always there, and we always keep them ready to use.*

Life is a long series of learning to use tools. While many tools are literal, there are also plenty locked away inside your brain waiting to be picked up and used. The distinction between *giving* someone tools and *showing* someone tools is subtle but distinct: The tools to deal with anything life throws at you are already there, just waiting to be mastered.

As Georgetown University's Lisa Directo-Davis describes it, "If you can point to any skill in your life that you have already mastered, it's literally just increasing your awareness and capacity for that thing. Even brushing your teeth."

If you are capable of brushing your teeth, then you already have a wonderful set of tools ready for use. Some tools come ready to use (children and Marines alike can figure out how to use crayons with little to no instruction). Others require some training.

In the case of loneliness, tools exist for that too. Power tools, in fact. The type of instruments that can take something with the potential to cause depression, anxiety, and self-destruction and turn it into a deep wellspring of creativity and inspiration. In the worst-case scenarios, having a toolkit can at the very least be the key to merely surviving.

In 1959, James Bond Stockdale was finishing up a master's degree in international relations at Stanford University. A career Navy officer and a seasoned fighter pilot, Stockdale was not particularly enthusiastic to learn about political science and diplomacy. Instead, he found himself gravitating to the philosophy corner of Stanford's campus, where he was able to study and learn about the human condition—a much more interesting subject.

Despite his cynical view of "military education," Stockdale graduated from Stanford with a master's of arts in international relations in 1962 and returned to the Navy to take command of a fighter squadron. Over the next three years he would deploy three times to the western Pacific as the US became increasingly involved in Vietnam. During his third deployment, now in the command of a Carrier Air Group of seventy aircraft, Stockdale found himself leading combat missions almost daily. On the morning of September 9, 1965, while flying at tree-top level returning from leading an attack on a railroad facility near the city of Thanh Hoa, his A4 Skyhawk light attack jet was hit by a North Vietnamese flak trap—a fusillade of antiaircraft fire which disabled his aircraft.[55, 56]

Fifty-seven-millimeter antiaircraft shells punched beer can-sized holes into the A4's tiny fuselage and stubby delta wings. With the control system of his aircraft shot out, the Skyhawk—one of the lightest, smallest, attack aircrafts in the US arsenal—caught fire. Stockdale reached up and yanked the bright yellow ejection seat handle above his head. The Douglass ESCAPAC ejection seat rocketed Stockdale out of the aircraft and into the sky. As his parachute opened, he gazed down at the North Vietnamese village below him and estimated it would be at least five years before he would see American soil again.[57]

This thought was interrupted by pistol fire, as rounds from below zipped through his parachute. Still partially inflated, the parachute hooked a tree, and Stockdale landed on the ground below without injury. No sooner had he released himself from his harness was he tackled by a dozen men from the village. The severe pummeling that followed continued unabated until a police officer arrived and dispersed the crowd.[58]

---

55  "Stockdale, James Bond," The National Aviation Hall of Fame, accessed August 25, 2020.

56  James Stockdale, *Courage Under Fire: Testing Epictetus's Doctrines in a Laboratory of Human Behavior*, Stanford, CA: Hoover Institution Press, 1993, 7.

57  Ibid.

58  Ibid, 11.

Suffering from a broken bone in his back and a dislocated knee, he was transported to the infamous Hoa Lo prison in downtown Hanoi (colloquially known as the "Hanoi Hilton"). Stockdale was the ranking officer among the approximately four hundred prisoners at Hoa Lo. He began organizing the prisoners, creating a system of support and solidarity to help them preserve their sanity and dignity.

The entrance to Hoa Lo prison.

Stockdale ended up spending nearly eight years as a prisoner of war in North Vietnam. During that time, he was denied food and medical attention, physically tortured, and kept in solitary confinement for four years (two of which were spent in leg irons).[59] His resistance against his captors came to a head on September 4, 1969, when, late at night in between torture sessions, Stockdale shattered a window and slit his own wrists to keep from giving up information on his fellow prisoners. He survived only because a wandering guard happened upon him unconscious in a pool of blood.

The North Vietnamese response was swift—Stockdale's action ended torture at Hoa Lo for all of the American prisoners held there. In 1973, Stockdale was released, where he returned to the United States and his family. In 1976, President Gerald Ford presented Stockdale with the Congressional Medal of Honor for his conduct while being held captive. In 1979, he retired from the Navy. After a brief stint as the president of The Citadel, he left to become a fellow at Stanford University's Hoover Institution on War, Revolution and Peace.

Throughout his ordeal at Hoa Lo, Stockdale often fell back upon his philosophy education at Stanford to sustain his mind. He thought particularly hard about lessons he had learned about the Stoics, a group of philosophers who believed in applying logic and reason to understand one's place within the natural world, rather than emotions or desires. At the Hoover Institution, Stockdale wrote and spoke extensively on the topic of Stoic philosophy.

---

59  Kate Lange, "Medal of Honor Monday: Navy Vice Adm. James Stockdale," *DoD News*, March 2, 2020.

One of Stockdale's essays, which I make a point of reading once a year, describes in detail how the teachings of Epictetus, a crippled slave in ancient Rome who later became a sought-after Stoic teacher, applied to being a prisoner of war. Epictetus eventually rose to philosophical prominence and became a secretary to Nero, the mad emperor who succeeded Claudius around the time the British Isles were being conquered. Stockdale's essay, "Courage Under Fire: Testing Epictetus's Doctrine in a Laboratory of Human Behavior," discusses how disciplined control of the mind helped Stockdale cope with the ghastly conditions he existed in for eight long years.

A good portion of "Courage Under Fire" focuses on the time prisoners spent in solitary confinement. Years later, one of the men imprisoned alongside Stockdale conducted a survey of the Hoa Lo prisoners, seeking to find out whether torture or isolation was a better mechanism for breaking the psyche. Of those surveyed, prisoners who were subjected to more than two years of isolation believed that isolation, more so than torture, was the key to long-term erosion of human purpose.

Stockdale himself describes it: "From my viewpoint, you can get used to repeated rope torture—there are some tricks for minimizing your losses in that game. But keep a man, even a very strong-willed man, in isolation for three or more years, and he starts looking for a friend—*any* friend, regardless of nationality or ideology."[60]

---

60  Stockdale, *Courage Under Fire*, 18.

Despite this, Stockdale persevered, understanding that his imprisonment, his torture, and his long stints of isolation were conditions outside of his control. He quotes Epictetus: "He who craves or shuns things not under his control can neither be faithful nor free, but must himself be changed and tossed to and fro and must end by subordinating himself to others."[61]

Why go on in the face of overwhelming odds? Years later, Stockdale's experience became encapsulated in an effect now referred to as the Stockdale Paradox. The paradox requires one to have unwavering confidence in success while approaching every obstacle in the present with a grim "worst-case" realism. Jim Collins interviewed Stockdale while writing *Good to Great*, which chronicles the journeys of companies and business leaders who topped their industries year over year. Similar to prisoners in the Hanoi Hilton, businesses that used Stockdale's Paradox fared better than those that held on to optimism that "things will get better... any day now." Stockdale defined his lesson to Collins thusly: "You must never confuse faith that you will prevail in the end—which you can never afford to lose—with the discipline to confront the most brutal facts of your current reality, whatever they may be."[62] Face reality head-on, but do not think for even a moment that you will not prevail in the end.

One of the most powerful tools to put into the toolkit for coping with loneliness is recognizing its condition and seizing control. Stockdale points out that, despite all of the things

---

61   Ibid, 9.
62   Jim Collins, *Good to Great*, (New York: Harper Business, 2001): 85.

in our life that are *out* of our control, a great many things are still *within* our control. Among them are aims, aversions, grief, joy, judgements, attitudes about what is going on, and understandings of personal good and evil.[63] Alain de Botton quotes a Senecan Praemeditatio, stating that "fortune gives us nothing which we can really own."[64] There is a reason that in depictions of the Roman goddess Fortuna she is holding both a cornucopia and a rudder. The cornucopia overflows with the best of what life has to offer, but the rudder symbolizes that she can just as easily change the direction of our life without warning. How we control our reactions when faced with the course that Fortuna has charted for us is what truly defines us, not the specific circumstances themselves.

Back in my training cell—a palatial accommodation compared to the Hanoi Hilton—I squat-sit on my cinder block. Time has lost all meaning, but I treat my current station in life with indifference. Not with contempt, only with indifference. Staring into the darkness, I crack a smile.

63   Stockdale, *Courage Under Fire.* 7.
64   Alain de Botton, *The Consolations of Philosophy,* (New York: Vintage Books, 2000), 91.

# DEFEAT

———

بِسْمِ اللهِ الرَّحْمٰنِ الرَّحِيْمِ *"For indeed, with hardship (will be) ease"*
— QUR'AN 94:5

In the spring of 1521, the kingdom of Navarre, modern-day Spain's northernmost border with France, was in disarray. A decade prior, King Ferdinand II had annexed Navarre, bringing the territory under Spanish rule and usurping the reigning House of Albret. The royal House of Albret was expelled over the Pyrenees Mountains into France.

Now, King Henry d'Albret, the son of the last king of Navarre before its annexation, was marching back across the mountains to retake the kingdom. Backed by the king of France, Henry crossed the Pyrenees with twelve thousand infantry, eight hundred knights, and twenty-nine pieces of artillery. The Navarrese people, unhappy under Spanish rule, rose up in support of Henry, bolstering the ranks of his army.[65]

---

65   James Brodrick, *Saint Ignatius Loyola: The Pilgrim Years 1491-1538*, (San Francisco, California: Ignatius Press, 1998), 56.

A recent revolt in the nearby Castilian territory had drawn all of the Spanish forces out of Navarre. When news of the invasion reached Navarre, the Spanish-installed viceroy recognized his vulnerability and dispatched a messenger to find one of his best knights, a Basque soldier named Íñigo de Loyola, known by the more common Latin interpretation of his name: Ignatius of Loyola. The viceroy's instructions were to proceed post-haste to Navarre's capital city of Pamplona to mount a defense. Ignatius was a career soldier with over a decade of distinguished service to the viceroy. Enlisting the aid of his older brother, Martín García, Ignatius rallied men from their family's estate and from around the province and raced to Pamplona.[66]

Earlier in the month Ignatius had helped to broker a shaky peace agreement with a local insurgency. However, once rumors of the Franco-Navarrese invasion had reached the city, the people were once again ready to rise against the Spanish occupiers. Ignatius, Martín, and Pedro de Beaumont, the commander of the Pamplona garrison, tried in vain to convince the citizens to help defend the city.[67] Facing insurmountable odds, a debate raged amongst the Spanish knights.

Martín, furious about the lack of reinforcements and the capitulation of the Navarrese citizens to the invading forces, voted to abandon the city. Ignatius fumed at Martín's lack of confidence. Standing opposite on the eve of battle, the two

---

66  Saint Ignatius of Loyola. *A Pilgrim's Journey: The Autobiography of Ignatius of Loyola*, translated by Joseph N. Tylenda S.J. (San Francisco, California: Ignatius Press, 2017), 37-38.

67  Ibid.

brothers glared at each other, each unwilling to compromise on their unassailable opinions.

Ignatius, a warrior to his core, believed surrender without any resistance was cowardice. It was the antithesis of the tales of the famous warriors that had enthralled him as a child. *The Song of Roland* didn't end in defeat—there, the Frankish army had died to the man but were avenged by Charlemagne and their enemy routed. A glorious end indeed. Ignatius outlined his plan for defending Pamplona, but Martín was unmoved. In the end, the brothers parted ways on the outskirts of the city, Martín leading the troops under his command back to their home territory, while Ignatius rallied the remainder to prepare the city. Unable to defend the entire town with the paltry garrison he was left with, Ignatius withdrew his forces to the fortress in the center of the town.[68]

The day was May 19—Pentecost Sunday—and Ignatius stood atop the imposing stone walls of the fortress of Pamplona, watching the Franco-Navarrese army descending down the hillsides to within artillery range. The few remaining citizens welcomed the invaders as they entered the city and began to surround the fortress on all sides.

Ignatius stared out at the sea of men, hard at work in the distance preparing for a siege. His reddish-brown hair blew in the spring wind, framing his hawkish face set atop the powerful yet compact body of a veteran soldier. What Ignatius lacked in height he made up for in zeal—both for Spain and his Christian faith. His aggressive personality and

---

68   Ibid.

courageousness inspired faith in the remaining defenders despite their dire situation. That evening, certain he would die in battle before surrendering and with no priests remaining in the fortress, Ignatius made an impromptu confession of his sins to another knight.[69]

As the sun rose the following morning, the French army began its bombardment of the Spanish garrison. Ignatius and his men took cover inside the castle as shells rained down around them. By the third day of the siege, the rest of the French troops had arrived and with them, heavy culverin cannons designed to punch through the fortress walls.[70]

Emboldened by their reinforcements, French soldiers charged the fortress as cannonballs flew overhead. The Spanish defenders, seeing they were on the verge of being overrun, raced to man the ramparts. Black powder smoke from the heavy arquebus muskets created a pale grey haze that rose up from the fortress. Ignatius, recognizing the severity of his men's predicament, ran from position to position, rallying their spirits.

As he ran between positions, an explosion showered him with debris and knocked him to the ground. Blinded with dust and searing pain, Ignatius tried to stand but could not summon the strength to his legs. Jagged fragments of gunstone and shattered brick surrounded him. He crawled over to his

---

69   Saint Ignatius of Loyola, *The Life of St. Ignatius of Loyola, Founder of the Jesuits*, ed. F. Francesco Mariani (London: Thomas Richardson and Son, 1847), 8.

70   Saint Ignatius of Loyola, *A Pilgrim's Journey: The Autobiography of Ignatius of Loyola*, 39.

rapier and grasped its damascened handle. Bright red blood mixed in with the ornate gilding of the Toledan hilt. Sword in one hand, he used the other to roll onto his back. Sitting up, Ignatius finally realized the severity of his wounds. His right leg had been shattered by a cannonball. Burning hot shrapnel from the impact had peppered his left leg.

Soldiers ran to his side, but the battle still raged around them. Ignatius masked his pain in a vain attempt to continue pushing his men forward, but the tide had turned against him. Seeing the carnage unfolding around them and the grievous wounds of their comrade, the Spanish defenders lost heart. The garrison faltered, and then surrendered entirely to the French attackers. Pamplona had fallen to the House of Albret.

Ignatius's legs were a bloody mess. The French soldiers discovered him lying stricken inside the fortress and carried him into the town below. Impressed by Ignatius's courage in battle, André de Foix, the French commander, showed compassion, even allowing the crippled warrior to be seen by military doctors. After assessing his wounds, the French decided he should be transported from Pamplona to his ancestral home in the nearby Basque province of Guipúzcoa.[71]

Overwhelmed with gratitude despite remaining in considerable pain, as a parting gift Ignatius gave his prized weapons and armor to the French doctors who had helped him. It was early June and Ignatius, still unable to walk, was transported in a litter by his fellow soldiers. In an effort to avoid French occupied territory, they navigated a circuitous route

---

71   Ibid, 40.

through the Basque countryside. Their caravan crossed over one hundred kilometers of mountains and valleys, stopping only briefly in the small Guipúzcoan town of Anzuola before arriving at Castle Loyola. Ignatius's arrival was met by Magdalena de Araoz, his elder brother Martín's wife. She immediately summoned local doctors and surgeons to begin work on repairing his mangled legs.[72]

The bones had been poorly set by the initial military surgeons, and the journey from Pamplona had only made the injuries worse. The only option was to break the leg again and reset the bones. Modern, scientific surgery using empirical and experimental approaches was still more than two centuries away. Despite a lack of contemporary anesthetics, Ignatius maintained his composure throughout the procedure, his military discipline and training taking over as the surgeons operated on him. The operation left Ignatius severely depleted. He could not eat or drink, and, expecting him to die within a matter of days, Magdalena summoned a priest to administer Ignatius's last rites.[73]

It was late June, and the feasts of Saints Peter and Paul were occurring. Deep in the darkness of that night, Ignatius's health turned around, and his body began to heal. As Ignatius's recovery progressed, it became apparent his right leg would never be the same, the bones having knit together unevenly leaving it shorter than the left. Once again surgeons were consulted and Ignatius, determined to return his body

---

72  Brodrick, *Saint Ignatius Loyola: The Pilgrim Years 1491-1538*, 59-60.
73  Saint Ignatius of Loyola, *A Pilgrim's Journey: The Autobiography of Ignatius of Loyola*, 41-42.

to as normal a condition as possible, demanded that the leg be removed.[74]

Ultimately, they reached a compromise, and his leg was opened back up so doctors could put the bones back into traction in an attempt to make it even. Weeks of excruciating pain followed, as each day his right leg was stretched with weights until it gradually became even with the left. Ignatius was totally unable to walk during his slow recovery. Immobilized, he sought out distraction through books. The selection in Castle Loyola was limited, and Magdalena provided Ignatius with Ludolph of Saxony's *The Life of Jesus Christ*.[75] The well-written fourteenth century scripture was a stark departure from the adventure novels Ignatius was used to reading, but left with nothing else to read, he dove deep into its pages.

This was also a time for deep introspection—a self-examination as it became more apparent to Ignatius that he would never return to combat. Daydreams of courage and valor on the battlefield only led to crippling disappointment. Stuck in bed for weeks on end, Ignatius closely examined his inner state, viewing his mental and emotional reactions to his daydreams from every angle of interpretation. Releasing himself from the desires and aspirations of his previous life allowed Ignatius to grow in new ways.

By the time he was able to stand, he was no longer the same person that had been struck down on the walls of the castle

---

74   Ibid, 42.
75   Ibid, 44.

of Pamplona. He was filled with "a consuming thirst for the greater truthfulness of mind and heart, a dread of illusion and self-deception, a moving sincerity and honesty in the endeavour to find his real self, the self known to God, the naked self."[76]

In early 1522, Ignatius traveled on a mule across Spain. His pilgrimage took him through the snowy Guipúzcoan highlands first to the sanctuary at Aránzazu, then to Navarrete to settle his affairs with the viceroy of Navarre. The viceroy paid Ignatius the full amount he was owed for the previous year's service. Ignatius used the money to pay off all of his outstanding obligations, then directed that the remaining ducats be used to refurbish a local shrine in Navarrete.[77]

Departing there, his journey took him to Santa Maria de Montserrat, the imposing Benedictine abbey chiseled high into the cliffsides of the Montserrat mountain range just outside of Barcelona. Inside the abbey, Ignatius knelt and laid down the last of his earthly possessions—the sword and dagger he had carried along his journey—at the feet of the legendary Catalonian "Black Madonna" statue, fasting and holding vigil in front of her for three days. As Ignatius let go of his weapons, he also released his claims to earthly possessions and aspirations, living only to serve his God.[78]

---

76 Brodrick, *Saint Ignatius Loyola: The Pilgrim Years 1491-1538*, 72.

77 Ibid, 74.

78 Saint Ignatius of Loyola, *A Pilgrim's Journey: The Autobiography of Ignatius of Loyola*, 60-62.

The Black Madonna at Montserrat. A wooden sculpture believed to have been carved in Jerusalem early on in Christian history.[79]

The transformation that occurred in the solitude of Ignatius's recovery would have impacts that reverberated around the world. He would go on to found the Jesuit religious order of the Catholic Church and was canonized as Saint Ignatius of Loyola in 1622, half a century after his death.

Ignatius recorded *Spiritual Exercises*, a compilation of meditations, prayers, and contemplative practices meant to discern the path one should walk through life. For centuries these exercises were most commonly practiced as a "retreat" of about thirty days in solitude and silence. While Ignatius framed his methods in the context of medieval Christianity, the concepts are ubiquitous across time, culture, and faith,

---

79   "Black Madonna at Montserrat: The Image of the Virgin Mary," Montserrat Tourist Guide, accessed October 7, 2020.

reflecting principles and techniques of introspection that can be used by anyone in a secular fashion.

Siddhattha Gotama (i.e., Buddha) reached his full spiritual awakening while sitting in silent meditation below the Bodhi tree. Seneca, the Stoic philosopher once said, "Nothing, to my way of thinking, is better proof of a well-ordered mind than a man's ability to stop just where he is and pass some time in his own company."[80] The Khalwati order of Islamic Sufis, founded in the fourteenth century in Herat, Afghanistan, centers its practice around the concept of *khalwa*, the act of total retreat for periods of up to forty days. Prehistoric Amazonian tribes have used Ayahuasca brews to isolate the human mind and connect it to "the affective life of the natural world."[81]

Across time and space, humans have tried to connect with the world and figure out what exactly all the fuss is about. Many, as in the case of Ignatius, have been spurred to conclusion by extraordinary circumstances. Most commonly, though, we discover our relationship with the world in the moments where we connect with ourselves. In places where we find ourselves isolated, stricken, and broken, we must keep in mind that it is all part of the process. Finding

---

80  Lucius Annaeus Seneca, *Letters from a Stoic*, translated by Robin Campbell (London: Penguin Books, 1969), 1.

81  Commonly known as Ayahuasca, Amazonians use a potent mixture of the woody vines of *Banisteriopsis* along with its conditioning partner, *Psychotria viridis*, to harness natural DMT in retreats designed to allow one to enter "transformative relations with larger organizing forces, with greater ecosystemic intelligences, which in turn tend to increase human self-consciousness, inspiration, revelation, and sense of mission." "Ayahuasca, Religion and Nature," *Ayahuasca.com* (blog), March 27, 2008, accessed August 27, 2020.

purpose is quite possibly one of the most important tasks we undertake in the short time we spend walking the Earth. Sometimes purpose is given to us, but rarely is it given freely. Retreat into yourself periodically, look deep into the random and cosmic times in which we exist, and perhaps a glint of purpose will reveal itself.

# TOOLS & REFLECTIONS

# PRESENCE

———

*"Everything up to the stepping out—there's actually no reason to be scared. And then in that moment, all of a sudden, where you should be terrified, is the most blissful experience of your life. And God placed the best things in life on the other side of fear."*

—WILL SMITH ON THE TOPIC OF SKYDIVING

How much of your life do you spend in the present moment? This was the question Andy Puddicombe asked a worn-down Richard Pierson in 2008 just as the pair was starting down the path that would eventually lead them to found Headspace.

"What a fantastic question," I mumbled to no one in particular as I stared placidly at the group of people sitting on the bench in front of me. Even if anyone was listening, no one would have heard me over the whining roar of the twin turboprops just outside the thin shell of the Viking Air DHC-6 "Twin Otter" aircraft.

Tufts of cotton-white clouds dotted an otherwise azure-blue afternoon sky. Far off in the hazy distance, Virginia's Blue

Ridge mountain range was barely visible. Emerald landscape framed the town of Orange, the location of James Madison's historic Montpelier residence.

The aircraft continued its climb, zigzagging first east, then west, then east again so as not to get too far from the airport. The bare metal frame shuddered as we climbed higher into the atmosphere. Then the world tilted sideways as we reached our cruising altitude, banked hard left, and began to whip back around. Two miles below me, a patchwork of farm fields covered the countryside; out the opposite window was an immeasurable blue abyss stretching toward the heavens. Inside, the seats had been ripped out to accommodate two long benches that ran parallel from fore to aft. Just fifty feet from nose to tail, the crowded Twin Otter was only slightly longer than Jim Stockdale's single-seat A4 Skyhawk. People straddled each bench, facing the rear of the aircraft where two or three more passengers sat huddled together on the floor.

The wings leveled off and the world righted itself. The pitch of the engines changed from a roar to a rumble and, for a brief moment, my center of gravity was thrown off balance as the aircraft slowed to a crawl through the sky.

"DOOR!" came a shout from the tail of the aircraft. The wiry man who had made the announcement was simultaneously grabbing a handle on the fuselage and yanking upward, pulling open a sliding door and revealing the plane's occupants to the rest of the world. Sunlight bathed the cabin and the engine noise, now no longer separated from the cabin, was cranked into hi-fi. Poking his helmeted head out into the wind and looking downward, the doorman nodded to three other passengers and then glanced at the cockpit.

Next to the door a glowing red light blinked off and a green one replaced it. A sense of urgency electrified the cabin as the man and two others scrambled fully outside of the plane, standing on the door's threshold and gripping a rail just inside. A fourth person gripped the chest straps of two of the outside men, forming a human ring, and gave them a hardy shake.

With an unceremonious whoosh, the group disappeared sideways out the door at a hundred miles an hour.

Everyone else in the cabin clambered over the benches, making their way toward the back of the plane. A duo in brightly colored jumpsuits set up facing each other in the threshold. With one synchronous step, they slid away from the airplane.

Now that I had moved closer to the door, the jumpers who had just exited were visibly shrinking as they fell away from us, bodies flying in perfect alignment, still facing each other as they disappeared from view.

I knelt at the door and gripped the rail above it. By now my head was fully out of the door staring down at the ground. Thin, chilly air splashed against my cheek and tugged at my face. Amidst the farmland I picked out a long, straight stretch of asphalt. Tracing my finger up the runway I located the drop zone almost directly below me. Tiny bright-white clouds broke up the geometric shapes of pastures and crop fields like milky ink spots over a sea of green.

All that remained in the cabin were me and a few skydivers harnessed to tandem passengers. The tandem jumpers—who had probably never ridden in an airplane with the door open, much less exited one from fourteen thousand feet—stared with blank expressions, too overwhelmed to even be nervous.

I had recently received my skydiving "A-License"—an official recognition of the fact that I knew just barely enough to fly unsupervised. Many people assume skydiving carries a great amount of inherent danger. The truth of the matter is it carries inherent *risk*, but far less danger than one might think.

In fact, for tandem skydiving (where you are attached to an experienced instructor), the US Parachute Association recorded only one fatality per five hundred thousand jumps *over the past decade*. The USPA explains that, based on statistics from the National Safety Council, "a person is much more likely to be killed getting struck by lightning or stung by a bee."[82]

But none of that was important in this present moment. Focusing on the tasks at hand erased any and all of life's doubt or uncertainty. Turning to face the doorway once again, I braced the muscles in my body for what was about to come next. Arms cocked at shoulder level, I launched off of my back legs out the door and was welcomed with a brief strong gust of wind, then weightlessness.

---

82  "Skydiving Safety," United States Parachute Association, accessed August 27, 2020.

I resist the temptation to grasp at the empty air around me, instead trusting that gravity will do all the hard work, and position my body belly-toward-the-earth. Everything that came before this moment and everything in the indeterminable future after vanished. The massive break up I had just gone through, the job I was starting next week, worries of the past and future all remained on board the aircraft as I dove away at a rate of one thousand feet every five and a half seconds.

In front of me the horizontal plane of the earth grew its share from the blueness of the sky. My arms remained at my shoulders with my hands framing my face. I dipped my right shoulder and turned ninety degrees. Leveling off, I dipped the other shoulder and turned back to my original heading. I threw my hands down toward my thighs. My torso followed, sending my body tumbling end over end in a front flip. Some simple fun in the sky.

By the time I reached five thousand feet, almost sixty seconds had passed, but I was time traveling—stretching each second out to twice its normal length as the panorama in front of me mainlined into my brain. The sparse clouds around me were almost eye level. My focus shifted from far to near as I checked the altimeter on my wrist. Numbers on the large digital display flew by. I was at my pull altitude. I bent both of my arms at the elbow, waving twice, before reaching back to grab the hacky sack at the bottom right side of the container on my back and tossing it out to my side.

The hacky was attached to a small pilot chute, which immediately caught in the wind, dragging the rest of my main parachute out of its pack. As nylon cells filled with air and popped open, my body's orientation to the earth went from parallel to perpendicular in a rapid hinging movement. With the canopy unfurled above me, the long front-to-back cells formed a wing. The hurricane winds dissipated, and I was suspended in silence.

Still alone, I reached up to grab the hand loop toggles that controlled the shape of the canopy. Removing them from their stow-location on the harness, I tested the toggles by pulling them down to my waist—first together, then separately, sending me in graceful spirals through the air. Satisfied, I let the left toggle all the way up while yanking the right one down to my waist, banking me so hard my ram-air parachute and I became fully sideways for a moment. Twirling around to face the airport, I began piloting myself back to Mother Earth.

You do not need to throw yourself out of an airplane to experience presence of mind. However, the importance of mindfulness even in everyday life cannot be understated. Skydive Orange has an entire blog post entitled "The Art of Keeping Calm," in which they explain how mindfulness practices purposely and purposefully bring attention to what is happening in the now and helps "garner control over the mind in a non-aggressive and non-judgmental way."[83]

Brian Germain, in addition to being a psychology researcher, author, and teacher, is a world-champion skydiver and parachute test pilot. In his book *Transcending Fear,* he speaks at length about the mind's ability to perceive and overcome fear.

He describes that in-the-moment feeling of presence as "flow." Other psychologists have termed it "flow state," and most people refer to it as being in the "zone." In Germain's words, "Flow is the space in which we let go of our worries, and dive deeply into the world around us. It is complete acceptance of what is going on, and complete cooperation." He likens it to learning to ski; fear causes new skiers to lean back toward the mountain, throwing them off balance and out of control.[84] As a person who learned to ski as a fully grown adult, I can verify this to be true.

The same holds true for exiting an airplane for a skydive. At the beginning of the Accelerated Free Fall (AFF) program, the prerequisite to earning a skydiving license, students are

83   "The Art of Keeping Calm," *Skydive Orange* (blog), January 30, 2020, accessed August 27, 2020.

84   Brian Germain, *Transcending Fear: The Doorway to Freedom,* (Rockville, Maryland: Adventure Wisdom LLC, 2013), Kindle location 1026-1068.

taught to face forward toward the front of the airplane, look up at the wing of the aircraft, and sidestep out the door on a timed count. On exit, the skydiver assumes an arched position as their body levels out.

Occasionally, as soon as they are out of the door, new skydivers will wriggle their bodies and flail their arms and legs as if they are grasping for something to hold on to. Their minds are existing in some past or future state—one where they are standing upright on solid ground and not flying at 120 miles per hour. As a result, they ignore the actions that need to be taken in real time. "The secret to surviving as a modern human lies in finding the way to fly, rather than fall," Germain states.[85]

"People often tell me that the reason they have never tried skydiving is because they are worried that they will freak out and neglect to pull their ripcord. Are you kidding? When there is a huge planet racing up at you, there is nothing else to think about. If you relax and keep your head, the next move becomes incredibly obvious."[86]

In his book *Green Light Your Life*, Germain offers his thoughts on the concept of presence: "By allowing yourself to collect mental resources in the present moment, you connect with the part of yourself that is completely peaceful and content. This is your basic self—secure and at ease."[87]

---

85   Ibid, Kindle location 91.
86   Ibid, Kindle location 1091.
87   Brian Germain, *Green Light Your Life: Awakening Your Higher Self*, (Rockville, Maryland: Adventure Wisdom LLC, 2013), Kindle location 2341.

Flow is not an idea exclusive to extreme sports. Joseph Gordon-Levitt describes the reason he loves acting so much as "being able to pay attention to just one thing." In a TED Talk, he rails against the "attention economy" that dominates so much of our time. He argues that seeking recognition is a detriment to creativity.[88] Scott Barry Kaufman, scientific director for the Imagination Institute, describes to HuffPost that "when in flow, the creator and the universe become one, outside distractions recede from consciousness and one's mind is fully open and attuned to the act of creating."[89]

Where do you find your flow state? Research has found an association between flow and conscientiousness, sharing positive relationships with variables such as "social problem solving, life satisfaction, subjective happiness, positive affect, and intrinsic motivation."[90] A separate study examines the relationship between flow and mindfulness, positing that they are antithetical due to the mental space each state occupies, however conceding in the discussion that "engaging regularly in mindfulness practice might ultimately increase flow ability, by helping to 'sweep out the mental cobwebs' that prevent people from entering flow states, and/or by teaching people to concentrate in single-minded ways that contribute to flow states."[91] Indeed, something is meditative and

88 "How craving attention makes you less creative | Joseph Gordon-Levitt," *YouTube*, uploaded by TED, 12 September 2019.

89 Scott Barry Kaufman, "The Creative 'Flow': How to Enter That Mysterious State of Oneness," *HuffPost*, January 25, 2012.

90 Ibid.

91 Kennon M. Sheldon, Mike Prentice, and Marc Halusic, "The Experiential Incompatibility of Mindfulness and Flow Absorption," *Social Psychological and Personality Science*, vol. 6, 3, (November, 2015): 276-283.

peaceful about sitting in an airplane immediately prior to kicking the brain into high gear as I step out of the door and enter the dive flow. Likewise, taking a moment to clear the cobwebs before putting pencil to paper, before playing the first note of a tune, or before entering that high-stakes meeting can frame our minds in a more fully present way, allowing us to become one with the universe and crush our day to day.

***

**A BRIEF NOTE ON MINDFUL INTROSPECTION:**
How can we practice being more present in our daily lives? Do we need to throw ourselves out of an airplane? Hardly. Presence of mind is not a new concept. Buddhist monks mastered mindfulness more than two millennia prior to today's mindfulness movement. "Buddhist scholars regularly point out that the word translated into English as 'mindfulness' (*sati* in Pali, *smriti* in Sanskrit) has 'remembering' as its fundamental meaning," Jack Petranker writes in an article for *Tricycle: The Buddhist Review*. "This is 'mindful presence'—presence that remembers. And to be clear, 'remembering' here does not just mean remembering to be mindful: it refers instead to remembering what has value, what matters most."[92]

---

92  Jack Petranker, "The Present Moment," *Tricycle* (blog), Winter 2014, accessed August 27, 2020.

I have dug through as many historical accounts as I could reasonably find and can decidedly say Ignatius of Loyola was not a skydiver. That being said, in the sixteenth century Ignatius developed his own system for mindful presence in the form of a Daily Examen, which practicing Jesuits perform twice a day. I have adapted Ignatius's five-step Daily Examen below into a secular mindset exercise that anyone can practice in about three minutes:

### 1. Presence
*Seek out a place of quiet and repose. Focus on your immediate surroundings and passively absorb the sights, smells, and sounds you encounter.*

In the early morning hours as I sit in my kitchen, Andy Puddicombe's calming English voice speaks to me: "Eyes open... nice soft focus... take a few deep breaths... in through the nose... out through the mouth...." A simple breathing exercise, it is a tool I can take with me everywhere I go. Even in the busiest metropolises of the world, take stock of your surroundings—places to sit undisturbed for a moment of escape exist more than you might initially think.

### 2. Gratitude
*Reflect on your favorite moment of the past day. Even in times when everything else is going wrong, consider that waking up and breathing is in itself a privilege and can be celebrated.*

A phrase I often find myself repeating is, "There but for the grace of God go I." The origin of the phrase is attributed to John Bradford, an English Reformer and contemporary of Ignatius. If that's too pious for you, next time you see misfortune in the world try saying out loud, "It could be me." Simple statements of humility instantly fill us with gratitude for the life and privileges we have.

### 3. Review
*Recall your emotions, thoughts, and urges of the past day. What are they telling you? Imagine them as objects you can turn and examine from every angle. What do those same emotions, thoughts, and urges look like flipped on their heads?*

Having been raised Catholic, I still (occasionally) enjoy the observation of Lent, the practice of sacrifice leading up to the Easter celebration, as a means of reflection and introspection. Several years ago, I chose to "give up" complaining for Lent. This turned out to be easier said than done, since that year Lent happened to fall on the period of time that I was going through both survival school and amphibious training, suffering innumerable injustices at the hands of instructors, weather, and the general breakneck pace of intense military training.

Not complaining became an exercise in creativity. What was a constructive way to voice an opinion? Did complaining about sleeping out in the pouring rain make me any less wet? When something goes wrong, no matter what it is or who is at fault, how can I change my perception of it to be a good thing?

### 4. Forgiveness
*Wipe your slate for the day. Whatever physical, mental, or moral failures you may have encountered in the past twenty-four hours are now merely lessons to inform your future self.*

Franciscan Monk Rohr observes in his book *Falling Upward*, "The general pattern in story and novel is that heroes learn and grow from encountering their shadow, whereas villains never do."[93] In a similar vein, thoughtful reflection on and acceptance of where you have failed should lead to growth. How can taking ownership of today's failures inform tomorrow's successes? Take this mindset to the extreme to build muscle memory—was I thirty minutes late to work because of traffic (an event over which I have no control)? Or was I late because I failed to *plan* for traffic (a thing over which I have absolute control).

In a TED Talk relating the story of a major operational failure in Iraq, Navy SEAL Jocko Willink challenges the audience: "Take ownership of everything in your world, the good and the bad. Take ownership of your mistakes, take ownership of your shortfalls, take ownership of your problems and then take ownership of the solutions that will get those problems solved."[94]

### 5. Hope
*The indeterminable future will be what you make of it. Make it good.*

Rohr points out: "Most people do not see things as they *are*; rather, they see things as *they* are."[95] Put to me another way by a hulking Marine special operations instructor pacing the

---

93   Richard Rohr, *Falling Upward: A Spirituality for the Two Halves of Life*, (San Francisco, California: Jossey-Bass, 2011), 131.
94   "Extreme Ownership | Jocko Willink | TEDxUniversityofNevada." *YouTube*, uploaded by TEDx Talks, 2 February 2017.
95   Richard Rohr, *Falling Upward*, 148.

selection barracks' rope corral before the start of a grueling ruck march: "Nothing in life is good or bad, only the way you think of it." A recruiting slogan for Marine Special Operations is "today will be different." It is up to you to make it so.

# BOREDOM

———

*"Tout le malheur des hommes vient d'une seule chose, qui est de ne savoir pas demeurer en repos dans une chambre" "All of men's unhappiness comes from one thing, which is not knowing how to stay at rest in a room."*
—PASCAL, PENSÉES, DIVERTISSEMENT 1670

Boredom is one of the hallmarks of the sea service, particularly those soldiers-of-the-sea we more commonly refer to as Marines. Unlike the action movies and TV shows I grew up with, the good guys did not embark from their homes, solve the world's problems, and heroically return in the span of an hour (with time for commercial breaks). I will never claim that I was sold a bill of goods about the Marine Corps, but the truth of the matter is that standing around for hours in the pre-dawn darkness waiting for the armory to open so I could retrieve my rifle does not exactly make for entertaining television.

Instead, Marines will train for months and then deploy for anywhere from six months to a year. Many portions of both training and deployment are spent unplugged—either far away at sea or in remote parts of the world with limited connectivity to the outside. While there will be moments of excitement, fear, joy, and sadness, for the average service member, these will be sandwiched between long periods of sheer boredom.

Most moments of boredom in the Marine Corps involve throwing rocks, explicit doodling, or some sort of physical competition. Some personal favorites include dragging each other through the snow on a skimboard towed behind a car, hunting care-package-stealing mice with night-vision goggles and blowguns, and using Composition C2 sheet explosive to blast our unit's logo into a piece of metal.

Fun fact: Boredom and deployment pets go together like peanut butter and chocolate.

An interesting social psychology paper published in 2014 entitled "Just think: The challenges of the disengaged mind" begins with a quote from John Milton's *Paradise Lost*: "The mind is its own place, and in itself/ Can make a Heav'n of Hell, a Hell of Heav'n."[96] This is Milton's way of saying, "It is what you make of it."

For the paper, researchers from the University of Virginia and Harvard University designed a study requiring participants to spend time by themselves, alone in their thoughts, in an empty room for periods of six to fifteen minutes. Participants left all of their belongings such as cell phones, books, and writing tools outside of the room. Their only instructions were to remain seated and not fall asleep.

Neural activity during such inwardly directed thought is called default-mode processing. The questions these researchers sought to answer were: "Do people choose to put themselves in default mode by disengaging from the external world? And when they are in this mode, is it a pleasing experience?"[97]

Not only did the results show that most people have difficulty concentrating when alone with nothing to do, but on average, participants did not enjoy the experience either. In fact, during one portion of the study, researchers demonstrated that participants would elect to receive negative stimulation over no stimulation. These participants were delivered an uncomfortable electric shock at the beginning of the study

---

96  Timothy D. Wilson et al., "Just think: The challenges of the disengaged mind," *Science*, 345 (July 2014): 75.

97  Ibid.

(uncomfortable to the point that they would pay money not to experience it again), and then given the same instructions to entertain themselves with their own thoughts. The participants were given a button that, when pressed, would deliver the same electric shock as before and then were left to their own devices.

Many participants decided negative stimulation was preferable to no stimulation: 43 percent of participants shocked themselves at least one additional time during the isolation period.[98] Artist and former Marine Lance Corporal Maximilian Uriarte, creator of the "Terminal Lance" comic strip, confirms this in one of his early comics describing the boredom of standing post (i.e., standing guard on deployment). Max jokes about the stages of boredom while on post, beginning with mundane conversation and eventually leading to singeing one's body with a lighter. In case such extreme escalation seems like hyperbole, he goes on to explain in his blog, "This actually happened at least three times that I can recall while on my first Iraq deployment."[99]

Jokes aside, much research is being done today to help alleviate the anxious and unpleasant feelings that come from feeling bored. Manoush Zomorodi, host of the WNYC "Note to Self" podcast and author of *Bored and Brilliant: How Spacing Out Can Unlock Your Most Productive and Creative Self* believes that beyond the initial unpleasantness lies

---

98  Of note, one outlier was not included: a participant who administered a whopping total of *190 shocks* to himself during the thinking period! Ibid, 76.

99  Maximilian Uriarte, "Terminal Lance #41 "Standing Post: Stages of Boredom," *Terminal Lance* (blog), June 8, 2010, accessed August 28, 2020.

a reservoir of creativity. In an interview on journalist Julia Bainbridge's "Lonely Hour" podcast, Manoush points out that our neurological network lights up when we allow our minds to wander. "That's when you do the deeper thinking," she explains.[100]

But the smartphone era has robbed us of our boredom, accelerating the speed at which information can be accessed for better or worse. No longer does a moment have to pass without entertainment. I can now use social media to see what my friends are doing in between checking emails, all while walking my dog.

Manoush argues that these attempts to avoid boredom and increase productivity are draining, and that rather than multitasking to spend as little time as possible inside our own heads, we are actually *task switching*. "A decade ago, we shifted our attention at work every three minutes," Manoush states in her 2017 TED Talk. "Now we do it every forty-five seconds."[101]

What most people refer to as multitasking is actually task switching—a form of mental "juggling." In truth, for 98 percent of the population, there is no such thing as multitasking.[102] Instead, we are rapidly jumping from one task to another and back again to our own detriment. As

100 Julia Bainbridge, "Inner Lives: Why Boredom Leads to Creativity, with Manoush Zomorodi," July, 2019, in *The Lonely Hour*, produced by Julia Bainbridge, podcast, MP3 audio, 9:29.

101 "How boredom can lead to your most brilliant ideas | Manoush Zomorodi." *Youtube*, uploaded by Ted, 29 August 2017.

102 Maria Konnikova, "Multitask Masters," *The New Yorker*, May 7, 2014.

explained by the American Psychological Association: "Although switch costs may be relatively small, sometimes just a few tenths of a second per switch, they can add up to large amounts when people switch repeatedly back and forth between tasks." One researcher estimated that even brief mental blocks created by shifting between tasks can cost as much as 40 percent of someone's productive time.[103]

In 2015, five years into my Marine Corps career, I knew none of this.

"I don't normally recommend this, but you might want to get tested for attention deficit disorder," the psychologist across from me said, only half joking. I was sitting in a cramped office nestled inside a gym on Stone Bay, the small southern annex of Camp Lejeune, North Carolina, where Marine Special Operations is headquartered.

Psychological testing is a normal part of special operations and this was a routine meeting to go over the test results of The Attentional and Interpersonal Style (TAIS) inventory I had taken a week ago. TAIS was developed in 1976 by psychologist Dr. Robert Nideffer and is used "to measure the behaviorally defined concentration styles, and interpersonal characteristics" with the theory that attentional and interpersonal style are the building blocks of performance.[104]

---

103  "Multitasking: Switching costs," *American Psychological Association*, March 20, 2006, accessed August 29, 2020.

104  Robert M. Nideffer, "Reliability and Validity of The Attentional and Interpersonal Style (TAIS) Inventory Concentration Scales," In D. Smith & M. Bar-Eli (Eds.), *Essential readings in sport and exercise psychology* (pp. 265-277), Champaign, IL: Human Kinetics.

While TAIS found immediate use amongst sports psychologists in the 1980s, it is designed more as a general measure of performance relevant characteristics, the purpose being to identify an individual's interpersonal strengths and weaknesses. Since then, it has been adapted for use by organizations like Citibank, General Motors, Harley Davidson, and the US Special Operations Command.[105] In Marine Special Operations, team commanders complete the inventory to assess and hone their leadership styles.

Among the twenty characteristics that had been measured by the lengthy questionnaire I had filled out, internal distractibility and external distractibility were obvious outliers. Placed on a normal distribution of world-class performers, I was in the 94th percentile for internal distractibility and the 99.9th percentile for external distractibility.

This explained quite a few things throughout my life: why paying attention in math class was so difficult but reading a fantasy novel was not, the hundreds of pairs of goggles misplaced during swim team practice, all the times I had forgotten my lunch in the refrigerator before leaving for work. My mind churned constantly, bombarded from every direction by stimuli—and now I had a possible explanation.

---

105 "The Attentional & Interpersonal Style Inventory: Business Report Sample," *Enhanced Performance Systems*, accessed August 29, 2020.

Name: Bryan Crosson
Date: 9/23/2015
Comparison Norm: World Champions (All)

Enhanced
Performance
Systems

## TAIS PERCENTILE SCORES

| | Score | Percentile |
|---|---|---|
| Awareness | 13 | 31% |
| External Distractibility | 32 | 99.9% |
| Analytical / Conceptual | 19 | 59% |
| Internal Distractibility | 21 | 94% |
| Action / Focused | 22 | 47% |
| Reduced Flexibility | 28 | 73% |
| Information Processing | 48 | 77% |
| Orientation towards Rules and Risk | 25 | 88% |
| Control | 51 | 92% |
| Self-Confidence | 25 | 70% |
| Physically Competitive | 23 | 91% |
| Decision Making Style | 19 | 96% |
| Extroversion | 23 | 25% |
| Introversion | 28 | 87% |
| Expression of Ideas / Intellectually Competitive | 15 | 25% |
| Expression of Criticism & Anger | 13 | 60% |
| Expression of Support & Affection | 17 | 22% |
| Self-Critical | 6 | 50% |
| Focus Over Time | 21 | 90% |
| Performance Under Pressure | 23 | 74% |

The Attentional and Interpersonal Style inventory.

Attention deficit hyperactivity disorder, or ADHD, is one of the most commonly studied and diagnosed neurodevelopmental disorders, particularly in children and adolescents but also in adults. It is characterized by difficulty regulating attention (i.e., staying focused), increased impulsivity and risk-taking behavior, and excessive activity. Researchers hypothesize that part of the issue involves frontostriatal network abnormalities and low levels of dopamine transporter proteins required to properly activate the brain's reward centers. In 2016, the Journal of Clinical Child and Adolescent Psychology estimated that 9.4 percent of children are diagnosed with ADHD.[106] The National Institute of Mental Health estimated in 2011 that the adult prevalence was 4.4 percent.[107] According to an Israeli study published in 2019, ADHD could also very likely explain my comically bad handwriting (apologies to everyone whose copy of this book I signed).[108]

I was never tested for or diagnosed with ADHD and I probably never will be. However, being able to maintain an awareness of self and understand weaknesses is critical to both driving performance and generally enjoying life. While I was in the Marine Corps, I practiced exercises to improve my focus and developed systems to ensure that an otherwise highly distracted mind did not enter into a downward spiral of task switching. Intentional mindfulness, meditation, and introspection are all parts of this system and help tame what Buddhists refer to as the restless, unsettled "monkey mind."

In the past decade research has begun to focus on the link between boredom and ADHD. In her 2014 book, *The Elephant in the ADHD Room*, Letitia Sweitzer explains, "While the threat of boredom is indeed universal, it is especially

---

106 "Data and Statistics About ADHD," *Centers for Disease Control and Prevention*, October 15, 2019, accessed August 29, 2020.

107 "Attention-Deficit/Hyperactivity Disorder (ADHD)," *National Institute of Mental Health*, November, 2017, accessed August 29, 2020.

108 Rony Cohen et al., "Handwriting in children with Attention Deficient Hyperactive Disorder: role of graphology," *BMC Pediatrics*, 19 (December 10, 2019): 484.

prevalent, intense, problematic, and often unbearable for individuals with ADHD."[109]

Sweitzer goes on to say that such agitation at the thought of boredom produces "another kind of 'misfit,' the kind that throws off mundane and outworn norms to create inventions, art, humor, and initiatives that benefit society and to thrill the world with record-breaking sports achievements and performances in arts and entertainment."[110]

Similar to recognizing and reframing loneliness, boredom is an opportunity for something magical and creative rather than a passive state. Think back to the film adaptation of Norton Juster's childhood classic *The Phantom Tollbooth*, which taught us, "Don't say there's nothing to do in the doldrums."[111]

### BESIDES, YOUR ATTENTION IS A HOT COMMODITY THESE DAYS.

How much money is one minute of your attention worth? Take a moment and think about how you might calculate it. Is it your hourly earning rate divided by sixty minutes? What about your spare time? How much is that worth?

Once you have a number in your head, let's take a look at what one minute of your time is worth to a digital marketer. An April 2020 report from DataReportal shows that for the

---

109 Letitia Sweitzer, *The Elephant in the ADHD Room: Beating Boredom as the Secret to Managing ADHD*, (London: Jessica Kingsley Publishers, 2014), 17.
110 Ibid, 25.
111 *The Phantom Tollbooth*, directed by Chuck Jones, Abe Levitow, and Dave Monahan (1970; Culver City, California: MGM Animation/Visual Arts), VHS.

4.57 billion internet users across the world, the average total amount of time per day spent using the internet is six hours and thirty-nine minutes (i.e., 399 minutes).[112] Data from eMarketer.com shows that worldwide digital ad spend in 2020 will be $332.84 billion, projected to grow by an additional $50 billion in 2021.[113]

So, doing some quick math, $332.84 billion divided by 399 minutes means in 2020 digital advertisers will spend approximately $834,000,000 per minute. Divide that number by 4.57 billion people, and you wind up with a much more reasonable 18 cents per minute. On average in 2020, one minute of your time is worth eighteen cents to a digital advertiser.

If that number is much less than the original number you came up with—the number *you* believe your time is worth—take a moment to reflect on how much time you spend looking at ads on the Internet. Whether it is click banners, emails, or sponsored content on YouTube, Facebook, and Instagram, we are bombarded with marketing at almost every moment we are connected to the Internet.

This is not necessarily a bad thing. The way we interact with the Internet informs how we are advertised to, often resulting in targeted ads that can introduce us to new products or rising fashion trends or let us know when our favorite store is having a sale. Techniques such as behavioral retargeting and dynamic creative advertising are becoming so

---

112  "Digital 2020: April Global Statshot," *DataReportal*, April, 2020, accessed August 29, 2020.

113  Ethan Cramer-Flood, "Global Digital Ad Spending Update Q2 2020," *eMarketer*, July 6, 2020, accessed August 29, 2020.

accurate that digital marketing expert Scott Galloway muses, "I think Walmart and TikTok could potentially introduce this new field that I'm calling 'a-comm,' and that's 'algorithmic commerce,' which is basically zero-click ordering that's fulfilling and sending you products before you order them."[114] Such radical ideas are embraced by a rising movement of "Dataists"—people who believe that our complex world is not only made simpler but improved upon by the use of big data and how humans interact with it.

In his book *Homo Deus*, Yuval Noah Harari describes the movement as a data religion where "the value of any phenomenon or entity is determined by its contribution to data processing" and humans should do our part to enrich "the global data-processing system." Eventually through this data religion, Harari argues, algorithms will gain enough predictive power to be able to know what important life decisions we should make with greater accuracy than we could ever know on our own.[115]

Until we as a collective society reach that point, consider the time you spend *not* connecting with media and adding data points to the system as valuable time to work on your own internal algorithms.

---

114  Kara Swisher and Scott Galloway, "Tesla's 'Battery Day', the DOJ prepares for Google, and Scott's prediction on "algorithmic e-commerce," 25 September, 2020, in *Pivot*, produced by Vox Media, podcast, MP3 audio, 1:03:25.

115  Harari raises some great points about the demonstrated value of "big data." Through the efforts by large tech companies, contact tracing of COVID-19 quickly became a reality in 2020, allowing the devices we carry to measure our risk of exposure faster and more accurately than ever possible before. Imagine how many people would have survived the Black Plague if such a technology had existed in the 14th century. Yuval Noah Harari, *Homo Deus*, trans. by the author, (New York: HarperCollins Publishers, 2017), 372-402.

Here is a three-step method to increase the value of your time:

**Step one:** Unplug the phone charger next to your bed and move it out of arms reach. Across the room is ideal, but one room over is even better.

**Step two:** Spend ten dollars on a cheap digital alarm clock— the no-frills kind that does nothing more than read the time and wake you up when it's set to.

Bank of America's 2015 Trends in Consumer Mobility Report discovered that 71 percent of Americans sleep with their mobile phone in arm's reach. One in three millennials surveyed sleep with their phone either on their bed or *in their hand*.[116] An International Data Corporation study sponsored by Facebook found that 44 percent of Americans use their phone as an alarm clock.[117]

---

**But *now* what will I do before I shut my eyes?**

What was the title of that book you have been putting off starting? Now might be an opportune moment to give it a shot. One caveat from the blog of Tim Ferriss: "Do not read non-fiction prior to bed, which encourages projection into the future and preoccupation/planning. Read fiction that engages the imagination and demands present-state attention."[118]

---

116  "Trends in Consumer Mobility Report 2015," *Bank of America*. 2015, accessed August 29, 2020.

117  "Always Connected: How Smartphones and Social Keep Us Engaged," *IDC*, 2013, accessed June 20, 2020.

118  Tim Ferriss, "Relax Like A Pro: 5 Steps to Hacking Your Sleep," *The Tim Ferriss Show* (blog), January 27, 2008, accessed August 29, 2020.

**Step three:** Set your phone alarm to go off thirty minutes after your new alarm clock. *Avoid touching any electronics from the time when your alarm clock goes off to the time your phone alarm goes off.*

In the same Bank of America report, 35 percent of respondents reach for their cell phone first thing upon waking up. That takes priority "ahead of coffee (17%), their toothbrush (13%), and even their significant other (10%)."[119]

Just like that, you have carved out thirty minutes that can be spent meditating, exercising, reading, writing, cooking, drawing, thinking, and creating. Most importantly, it is thirty minutes of time uninterrupted by messages, emails, that news alert you almost definitely will not click on anyway, or any other electronic interference.

If reaching for your phone and checking messages is currently your first task of the day, *Forbes* has some thoughts for you: "To reduce stress and enhance productivity, it's critically important to start mornings in the driver's seat—methodically and intentionally deciding how you'll allocate your time and energy," writes senior contributor Dana Brownlee. "Obsessively monitoring email can too often sabotage our ability to do that."[120]

---

119 "Trends in Consumer Mobility Report 2015," *Bank of America.*

120 Dana Brownlee, "This Dangerous Morning Habit May Sabotage Your Productivity All Day," *Forbes*, September 10, 2020.

**Beating Sleep Inertia**

Having difficulty getting up once that alarm goes off? You're experiencing the effects of sleep inertia—the medical community's term for that groggy period between sleep and wake. One solution: Try a sunrise alarm clock that gradually brightens the room before waking you up. Melatonin, the hormone responsible for regulating our sleep-wake cycle, is suppressed by bright light exposure. A paper published by researchers from the University of South Australia highlights the fact that "bright light exposure has also been shown to directly improve alertness and cognitive performance during the day, night, and following sleep restriction," going on to suggest that "there is potential for bright light exposure to directly improve alertness and performance during the sleep inertia period."[121]

Even better, research shows that unplugging for a bit before bed will improve the quality of your sleep. Researchers from Cornell University and the University of Washington "found social media and communication apps also interplayed significantly with behaviors before and during sleep, with over 50 percent of sensed sleep interruptions corresponding to social media app use alone." Even participants in the study who turned their phone facedown to avoid sleep interruptions were occasionally awakened by "phantom notifications."[122]

Leaving your electronics out of arm's reach at night removes the temptation to spend that hour staring at your screen before bed, or the temptation to wake up and open up

121  Siobhan Banks et al. "Time to wake up: reactive countermeasures to sleep inertia," *Industrial Health*, 54 (November 2016), 528-541.

122  Elizabeth L. Murnane et al. "Mobile Manifestations of Alertness: Connecting Biological Rhythms with Patterns of Smartphone App Use," *MobileHCI*, 16 (September 2016), 465-477.

Instagram just to spend the next twenty (or more) minutes scrolling. Go analog for a bit—the Internet will still be there in thirty minutes.

The caveat of course is for those professionals who are "on call" and who require rapid access to their device. But if that is not you, keeping your mornings and evenings free from intrusion is the first step to making your time more valuable. After all, those first thirty minutes of the day *are only worth $5.48 to an advertiser.*

# ANALOG

---

*"The first rule of knife fighting is to plan on getting cut."*
—ADVICE FROM A CHIEF WARRANT OFFICER GUNNER DURING
THE MARINE CORPS INFANTRY OFFICER COURSE, CIRCA 2011

"He's got a knife!"

A short, mean-looking Thai man stood in the dark, ankle-deep ocean and glared at me. Shocks of straight black hair fell across his tanned forehead, settling over a furrowed brow and two almond eyes gleaming with a combination of anger and fear. Shimmering reflections of the moon in a sapphire night sky pulsed in the ripples around our ankles. One hand was tucked behind the man's back as his gaze shifted between me and my Canadian acquaintance, whom I had met earlier that afternoon.

With a silent nod of approval, we lunged forward from two angles, rushing the man and tackling him into the slack water. Keeping him pinned under our body weight, I squeezed my hand around his trunk and gripped his fist. I strained to pry his fingers apart until I felt a rough wooden handle. Shifting my weight to twist the man's body away from his arm caused him to fully release his grip. I snatched the handle in my hand and stood, examining the fixed-blade razor I now possessed.

The three of us struggled for control in the warm, shallow tide pool. Beads of sweat and saltwater made gaining the upper hand a difficult task. Finally, I managed to put the man into an improvised hammerlock, with his arm cocked behind his back. Psychologist David Allen Grossman posits that the "fight-or-flight" response can really be broken down into "fight, flight, posture, or submit."[123] I did not want to hurt the man who was now squirming under my knee, but I sure as hell was not going to give him the chance to hurt me either. Now was the time to posture. *You robbed the wrong tourists, buddy.*

Earlier that day I had arrived in Thailand and jumped on a ferry out to a small chain of islands in the Andaman Sea. Traveling alone, I quickly made friends with some other like-minded travelers and proceeded to celebrate our newfound friendship with a trip to the bars. Three bars and one amateur Muay Thai fight later, our newly formed group decided to go for an ocean swim. As we waded into the bay, the light and noise of the beach bars gradually faded, overtaken by moonlight and the rhythmic lapping of nearshore waves.

The water was temperate and welcoming, and a gentle wind cooled the otherwise humid atmosphere. Empty long-tailed boats bobbed around us, anchored in place for the night.

---

123 Dave Grossman, *On Killing*, (New York: Back Bay Books, 2009), 7.

Their rudimentary Weedwacker-esque driveshafts hung over the stern, giving them the appearance of shadowy horned beasts. The land around the bay formed a U-shape, no more than a thousand yards wide, that stretched around us like protecting arms, keeping the dark sea at bay. Jagged cliffs climbed for hundreds of feet out of the jungle and up each of the arms.

Upon returning to the beach, we discovered a man digging through the pile of belongings we had left on the shore. Startled by our emergence from the water, he tore off into the darkness. Me and one of the other men in our group—the Canadian—chased after him. The island, with a size less than four square miles and a population of about three thousand people, did not leave many places to hide. With no cars or drivable roads, our foot chase led us in circles through a narrow maze of resorts, bars, hostels, and tattoo parlors.

The thief, eager to lose us, doubled back toward the beach, gaining a pair of companions who ran with him out into the low tide. Their silhouettes tore across the shallow bay. By now the water only came up to our calves, and we struggled through the soft sand as we followed the thieves away from the shoreline. The previously bobbing boats now rested on soft sand, their keels tilting them on a gentle kilter. The trio scrambled into one of the larger boats, a twenty-five-foot cruiser, and took shelter in the cabin at the boat's fore. As we approached, they emerged from below deck to confront us.

The ensuing melee had brought us to the present moment, my Canadian friend pinning one of the would-be thieves to the ground while I stood and faced the other two, who had armed themselves with hammers from below deck.

The standoff ended when we agreed to release the man in the water and the rest of our group arrived with two local police officers. When all was said and done, none of our property was recovered. I was less than twenty-four hours into a new country and now without a phone and missing half of my credit cards.

Fortunately, I had an old tablet and my passport locked up back in my hostel room, so I was not totally out of pocket. But my primary connection to the rest of the world—my phone—was gone for good.

Undeterred by my initial impression of Thailand, I spent the next week exploring the island. I walked about untethered from electronics. Once the initial anxiety of being offline abated, I thought about comedian Louis CK's bit about how parents spend more time recording their children's dance recitals than they do actually watching them. Liberated from the need to whip out my phone to document and upload every moment, I soaked up the unfiltered world around me.

You never realize how much life is spent scrolling through the lives of others until you are severed from your modern means of connection. I still had a digital single-lens reflex camera and a tablet on which I could type and journal the things I saw, but these were tools, not distractions.

With more attention focused on the present, the sights, smells, and sounds of Southeast Asia became even more vivid. Rows of reddish-ocher chicken satay sizzled over beds of glowing embers on street-side grills, wafting fragrances of garlic and lemongrass into the air where they mixed in the moist petrichor breeze with benzene from the passing road traffic. The buzz of the developing world was a wedding of the traditional and the contemporary that swallowed me whole. Simple experiences such as wandering lost through Chiangmai's garment district in search of ikat silk or eating wild mangoes and spicy fish paste on the side of the street with an old woman and her family became privileged experiences made possible by having both eyes focused on the world around me.

One week after losing my phone, I walked across the border between Thailand and Laos and boarded a "slow boat" to take me down the Mekong River from the border town of Huay-Xai to the ancient town of Luang Prabang. Here along the primitive riverbanks of the lower Mekong basin I was not only disconnected from my own personal world but from the rest of civilization in general.

The slow boats used in Laos are essentially hundred-foot river freighters converted to hold passengers. They are fitted with a wooden roof and have rows of seats installed from fore to aft with an aisle down the middle much like a passenger plane. They have no assigned seats, and locals and tourists alike use the boats as a means of efficient transportation across the country. The trip from Huay-Xai to Luang Prabang would take two days, with an overnight stop in Pakbeng, a curious hillside town located on a bend in the river.

A Laotian slow boat on the Mekong River.

Creative boredom filled the hours of placid floating between sparse grass-hut villages carved out of the jungle. I snapped photographs and journaled. I reread *Heart of Darkness*, wondering if Conrad's controversial novella on colonialism in Africa would spark some introspection into my own journey only to realize I had clearly conflated the text with my memory of Francis Ford Coppola's *Apocalypse Now*. Finally, as my boredom reached its apex, I began to write.

I had a pile of undeveloped ideas for short stories scrawled into my notebook and piling into the Notes app on my tablet. As our boat continued its creep downriver toward Luang Prabang, I converted one of my story ideas, a mission in Afghanistan I had been struggling to put to paper, into a short poem. Two years later the poem was published in an anthology of veteran poetry (Dead Reckoning Collective's *In Love... &War*)—a minor but significant victory for a Marine with no real writing experience ("The few, the proud, the laughably bad spellers").

## WHY DO WE HAVE SOME OF OUR BEST IDEAS WHILE FOLDING LAUNDRY?

My experience unintentionally replicated an experiment that Manoush Zomorodi posed to her listeners in 2015. She created a series of "Bored and Brilliant" challenges (the challenges would go on to inform her eponymous book). Each challenge focused on a different aspect of everyday life that is impacted by smartphone usage. Whether snapping thousands of pictures, compulsively checking and rechecking email, or scrolling through social media, Manoush hypothesized that life would be better with a little less screen time.

The final challenge, which is included in Manoush's book, is executed in three steps. First, reflect on an aspect of life that you want to improve but for some reason have avoided. Second, get bored. Really bored. Manoush recommends hiding every device or distraction and taking up an activity like watching water boil or writing tiny ones and zeroes from the top of a piece of paper to the bottom. Finally, after the mind is effectively numbed, return to the original problem in step one and attempt to solve it.[124]

Through the momentum of sheer boredom, "you will bring new creativity and focus to whatever subject you've chosen,"

---

124 Manoush Zomorodi, *Bored and Brilliant: How Spacing Out Can Unlock Your Most Productive and Creative Self*, (New York: St. Martin's Press, 2017), 162-163.

Manoush explains. "The goal is to use boredom to unlock a brilliant solution to your problem."[125]

To be clear: You do not need to get into a fight with knife-wielding thieves in Thailand to unlock your innermost creative self. You never know when you will strike boredom and be blessed with an opportunity for creative thought. I have sketched elaborate drawings in the back of staff meetings (sorry, boss) and penned silly haikus on the side of Mount Kilimanjaro.

Think about the adult coloring book craze that took hold in 2015. What makes such a simple task so soothing? Aside from psychological theories around color therapy, staring at a sheet of paper and mindlessly coloring between lines allows us to step into that deeper "default mode" for a bit and unlock a bit of creativity and tranquil self-expression. Johanna Basford, an illustrator and self-proclaimed "ink evangelist who prefers pens and pencils to pixels," states in an interview with Nikki VanRy, that "social media, smart phones, rolling news—all these things make us constantly connected to the world, never really focusing on something for an extended period time and always distracted by pings or notifications or screens."[126] Basford explains that "colouring gave people an accessible way to be creative and treat themselves to some digital detox time."[127]

125  Ibid.

126  Johanna Basford, "Johanna Basford," Johanna Basford's Personal Website.

127  Nikki VanRy, "What Happened to Adult Coloring Books? Charting the Boom and Bust," *Book Riot*, November 6, 2019.

The next time you are sitting around bored out of your mind, resist the urge to seek distraction by scrolling through your phone, tablet, or television. Instead, embrace the feeling and see where you wind up.

# STRUCTURE

---

*"Greatness can't be imposed; it has to come from within. But it does live within all of us."*

—*JEFF SUTHERLAND*, SCRUM: THE ART OF DOING

TWICE THE WORK IN HALF THE TIME

Now that we have established the creative benefits of boredom, how do we harness it? Being a relatively boredom-prone individual, I have come to the realization that the best way to leverage distraction is to build systems around it.

There is no shortage of goal-setting techniques people use to accomplish things that are personally important to them. Leaders and managers like to use goal-setting as a means to motivate the people under them. "Where do you see yourself in five years?" is a common question asked in job interviews as a gauge of one's vision of their future self. No matter who you ask, anyone who has achieved something worthwhile probably used some sort of goal-setting technique, even if they did not realize it. I will not wax poetics here on how people should go about attaining their goals, but I will relate a method that has worked for me.

When I was preparing to leave the Marine Corps and applying to business school, I enrolled in a few online courses on software development. I knew nothing about the world outside of the military. My only observation was that people I respected in the business world discussed the "tech industry" as if it was the world's most important development since ancient Sumerians invented writing in 3400 BC.

Without a single line of code in my lexicon, I struggled through a class on Agile software development. When I finished the course, my understanding about software development was only marginally better than nothing at all, but I had some new ideas on how to organize my life using a framework common in the software development community.

Scrum is an Agile technique created by Jeff Sutherland, a former US Air Force fighter pilot and serial tech entrepreneur. In 1967, Sutherland was flying reconnaissance missions over North Vietnam in a RF-4C Phantom jet. His unit, the 432d Tactical Reconnaissance Wing, "accounted for more than 80 percent of all reconnaissance activity over North Vietnam."[128] The squadron lost 50 percent of its aircraft to North Vietnamese air defenses in the course of one year, and at least one of Sutherland's fellow RF-4C pilots, John Stavast, was imprisoned alongside Jim Stockdale in Hoa Lo.[129, 130]

128 Douglas Withers, "Air Force 432nd Tactical Reconnaissance Wing," *Together We Served*, accessed 13 September 2020.

129 Jeff Sutherland and J.J. Sutherland, *Scrum: The Art of Doing Twice the Work in Half the Time* (New York: Currency, 2014), 24-25.

130 "Bio, Stavast, John E." *P.O.W. Network*, accessed 13 September 2020.

After the war, Sutherland achieved his master's in statistics from Stanford University (Stockdale's alma mater) and went on to become a professor of mathematics at the US Air Force Academy in Colorado Springs. After a brief period of time conducting scientific research for the Colorado Regional Cancer Center, Sutherland moved on to consult for various technology companies, all the while taking note of the inefficiencies of the software development cycles of the time. The synthesis of all of his observations eventually became Scrum.

Scrum is designed for small teams of developers to break large tasks into smaller goals that can be completed within a certain timeframe. These iterations are called *sprints* and usually are limited to two to four weeks. At the end of a sprint, the team holds a review of their progress and adjusts their future goals accordingly.

I combined the idea of a Scrum sprint with the Deconstruction principle entrepreneur Tim Ferriss uses for rapidly learning new skills (the full technique and all of its principles are described in detail in Ferriss's book, *The 4-Hour Chef*). The key question in Deconstruction is "What are the minimal learnable units, the LEGO blocks, I should be starting with?"[131]

Tim Ferriss uses this in the context of learning skills, but it is just as applicable to achieving goals. He has also referred

---

131 Timothy Ferriss, *The 4-Hour Chef: The Simple Path to Cooking Like a Pro, Learning Anything, and Living The Good Life* (New York: Houghton Mifflin Harcourt Publishing Company, 2012), 38.

to the method of deconstruction as "chunking."[132] Much has been written on the effect of setting goals that are too large. Because of the oft-fickle nature of the human mind, a goal that is too lofty can be the cause of intimidation, discouragement, and abandonment.

Running an Ironman race (a 2.4-mile swim, 112-mile bicycle ride, and 26.2-mile run) seems impossible if the farthest you have run in the past year is to the mailbox and back. This is the exact reason that six- to twelve-month training plans exist to iterate you all the way to the finish line.

In my case, I was preparing to exit the warm safety blanket of the Marine Corps and begin the life of a (f)unemployed broke grad school student within the next year. The first step was being admitted to a program. I picked up a blank notebook and wrote out this goal at the beginning of it. A study by psychology professor Dr. Gail Matthews of the Dominican University of California discovered that one is 42 percent more likely to achieve goals simply by writing them down.[133]

With these long-term goals in mind, I began taking ten minutes every Sunday evening and writing weekly sprints. I deconstructed each goal into its smallest possible components and then set objectives for each week. Starting small was a necessity—a curve comes with learning any new skill, and I knew early successes would allow me to build on the system I had created. Flipping through my notebook, numerous brief entries read things such as: "Three admissions

---

132  Alexa Albanese, "Tim Ferriss: How to Rig the Game So You Can Win It," *Creative Live*, December 9, 2016.

133  Gail Matthews, "Goals Research Summary," July 23, 2007.

**124 · THE LONESOME THREAD**

events added to my calendar, four application essays drafted, five hours of GMAT math studying...."

In the Marine Corps when you are not deployed, space throughout the day that is not occupied by the training schedule is called "white space." I was taught early on in my career that white space is an opportunity to chip away at whatever objectives I had for my team that would have otherwise fallen to the wayside. Rather than Marines reclining in the field throwing rocks at each other (a favorite pastime), this gap in the training schedule is an opportunity to improve the small things that I feel might have been underemphasized. Whether honing medical skills or programming radios, there are always opportunities to use white space productively.

So, what about white space in life? I reflected on the amount of vacuous time I have spent watching Netflix and playing video games. What else could that time have been spent doing? I ensured all of the weekly goals I wrote myself could be broken down into hour-or-less-sized chunks. They were written reminders of what to do with my personal "white space." Soon my notebook became attached to my hip. Rather than coming home from work and turning on my TV, I began opening my notebook and looking at what was on my weekly list.

Eventually I expanded the scope to encompass personal goals and form habits I thought would improve my life in general. Cooking new recipes, learning photography, writing creatively, and practicing yoga all found their way into my weekly sprints. Anything that popped into my imagination during that "default mode" autobiographical planning went into the notebook. Just like a Scrum sprint, at the end of each week I would review my progress and take note of anything I did not get accomplished. I would make an assessment of why I had missed the mark and then incorporate the lessons learned into the next week's goals, writing detailed notes at the bottom of the previous week's entry.

Reflecting on why a goal is missed is a crucial element of this technique, and it ties into a broader understanding of training our mind to effectively accomplish the goals we set for ourselves. Craig Weller, a former Navy Special Warfare Combatant-Craft Crewman (SWCC), explains why tempered reflection on failure is important in a blog entry for OAF Nation. He describes a "3R" drill, which is "a way of reliving past experiences to make them better examples of the skills we want to develop."[134]

The 3R drill is:

- Reimagine
- Revise
- Restore

My land navigation blunder during special operations selection was certainly momentarily panic inducing, but it was not crippling, and by acting quickly I was able to make a plan to get back on course. The reason? Because I had made similar mistakes a dozen times before over my career and *learned from them.* Each time, in Ignatian-like examen,

---

134  Craig Weller, "The Three Rs," *Hitter Feed* (blog), *OAF Nation*, August 6, 2020, accessed 22 September 2020.

I found ways to tweak my performance to improve. Do not skip over reflecting on why you missed the mark on a goal.

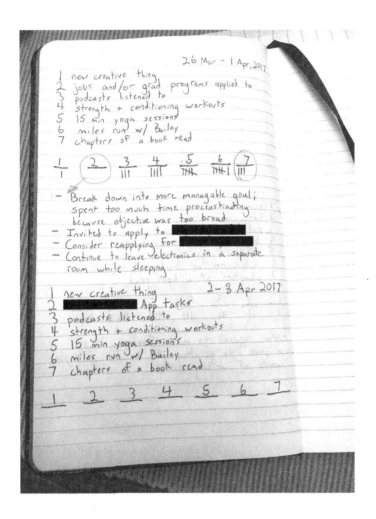

To make goals more accomplishable, a good principle to follow when writing them out is to use the well-known SMART acronym. First coined by George T. Doran in a 1981 issue of *Management Review*, SMART stands for Specific,

Measurable, Assignable, Realistic, and Time-related. Variations of SMART are commonly used in project or employee management, and the concept is easily adapted to everyday life.[135]

Weekly sprint goals should be Specific and Measurable—goals that I wrote that turned out to be too amorphous required me to spend as much time ideating on how to clarify them as I spent actually working toward them. Assignable, or who the goal is assigned to, in this case is obvious. Realistic and Time-related are connected; you must have a general idea of how much white space you will have over the next week. If I write a goal to lift weights four times in the next week, but I know my work schedule will not allow it, then it is not a realistic goal. This is also why I ultimately landed on one week as the length of my sprints—anything longer made my schedule and white space much more difficult to forecast.

Most importantly, *put your small goals on your calendar now.* Carve the future time out today. One thing differentiating goals that are achievable and goals that are merely aspirational are the actions taken toward them *today.* A weekly goal can be something as small as signing up for that scuba diving class you haven't found the time for yet. Making a new time commitment for the future can be a goal in itself.

---

135  "Smart Goals: How to Make Your Goals Achievable," *Mind Tools* (blog), accessed 11 September 2020.

### White Space: An Alternate Theory

In design, white space is an important concept closely related to the idea of using "negative space" to draw attention to specific elements. The business media publication *Fast Company* points out that white space between paragraphs and margins improves reading comprehension by up to 20 percent.[136]

If you want a good example of white space in design, look no further than the Google search page. The recognizable logo, search bar, and two simple buttons are surrounded by empty space, which draws the viewer's attention to the center of the page. This elegant design choice was originally at least in part to save on load times for users in the dial-up era of the internet.

White space in design reduces the cognitive load on the mind, allowing it to focus on what is important. In this context, white space can be thought of as those mindful practices we can use in spare moments of the day that center us and allow us to be more present in our work, recreation, and relationships.

## GOAL SETTING, TOP 10 JOYS, AND ELEMENTS OF INTEREST

Letitia Sweitzer advocates for a creative method of discovering what our individual goals should be. In an exercise she calls the "Top 10 Joys," Sweitzer has her clients go back in time, recall and relive their happiest moments, and write short entries describing each occasion that comes to mind. "Write down the ten occasions, events, or activities in your life that have given you the most joy or the greatest satisfaction or made you the happiest," she prompts. The language is important: Sweitzer points out that journaling

---

136 Jerry Cao, Kamil Zieba and Matt Ellis, "Why White Space Is Crucial To UX Design," *Fast Company*, May 28, 2015, accessed 11 September 2020.

happy *moments* causes clients to focus on a feeling, rather than simply ideating on random things they think are interests.[137]

From there, Sweitzer goes through each of the Top 10 Joys and asks her clients, "What about this made you joyful?" The responses she receives are then grouped into what she calls Elements of Interest. "After grouping them, you will see that the Top 10 Joys of some people are almost all about only one Element," she writes, "Ideally, an element will be repeated, verifying its importance. You may note that Joy and Interest are not the same thing by definition. However, what brings you joy will interest you, attract your attention, and draw you in."[138]

Sweitzer offers a (non-exhaustive) list of possible Elements of Interest:[139]

---

137  Letitia Sweitzer, *The Elephant in the ADHD Room: Beating Boredom as the Secret to Managing ADHD*, (London: Jessica Kingsley Publishers, 2014), 41-51.
138  Ibid, 42.
139  Ibid, 60-63.

| Acclaim | Control | Hands-on-interaction | Order | Sex |
|---|---|---|---|---|
| Action | Credit | Humor | Originality | Skill |
| Advocacy | Curiosity | Imagination | Physical action | Social interaction |
| Affiliation | Danger | Instant gratification | Predictability | Speed |
| Altruism | Design | Mastery | Problem-solving | Story |
| Applause | Drama | Multi-sensory experience | Purpose | Surprise |
| Certainty | Entrepreneurship | Nature | Rebellion | Suspense |
| Challenge | Exercise | Newness | Reveling in skill | Taste |
| Color | Exploration | Nonconformity | Rhythm | Texture |
| Competition | Face-to-face | Novelty | Risk | Time limit |
| Conflict | Facing-fear | Nurturing | Romance | Uncertainty |
| Contemplation | Fostering | Observation | Rule-breaking | Urgency |
| Construction | Group participation | One-on-one interaction | Scent | Variety |

So, what are the ten occasions, events, or activities in your life that have given you the most joy, greatest satisfaction, or happiest feeling? What about each event made you joyful? What would you consider to be *your* Elements of Interest?

Sweitzer uses this tool with her clients. However, it is also useful as a self-interview technique. While knowledge that the end goal is identification of a few Elements of Interest dilutes the exercise a bit, consider it a meta-analysis of what makes you tick. If scoring the winning goal of a high-stakes championship is one of your Top 10 Joys, *what about it made you so happy?* How can that inform your life today? More importantly, how can it inform your life *tomorrow?*

Build your personal goals around your Elements of Interest. I originally learned how to operate a camera in the Marine Corps for reconnaissance and surveillance missions, however I picked up photography as a hobby because some of the Elements that resonated with me included control, technical mastery, and creativity. Designing goals that capitalize on your interests makes them both more enjoyable and easier to accomplish.

We build systems to provide structure where none exists. In the programming world, system software is the necessary link between a computer's hardware and a user's applications. It is the layer that determines the basic functionality of a computer. In a similar way, designing effective systems to structure our time can be considered a building block upon which we can then add programming of our choice. Whether it is learning something new, working out, improving relationships with ourselves and others, or anything else, programming order into our own lives is the first step.

## My Top 10 Moments of Joy Are:

1. _____

2. _____

3. _____

4. _____

5. _____

6. _____

7. _____

8. _____

9. _____

10. _____

## My Top 5 Elements of Interest Are:

1. _____

2. _____

3. _____

4. _____

5. _____

**Long-Term Goals based on my Elements of Interest**

1. _____
2. _____
3. _____
4. _____
5. _____

**Week:** _____

Sprint goals based on my long term goals

1. _____
2. _____
3. _____
4. _____
5. _____

Notes: _____

_____

_____

_____

# CREATION
# & GRATITUDE

# PERFORMANCE

---

*"I don't find all this mindless activity one bit boring. I find it restful. The counting is a kind of meditation, an aquatic metronome that drives out all the internal flotsam. I leave the pool with a sense of well-being that carries me through the day."*

—SARA RIMER, "SWIMMING FOR FITNESS AND SOLITUDE,"

NEW YORK TIMES MAGAZINE, APRIL 29, 1990

The sun peeked over the horizon as a cool breeze blowing in over the peninsula electrified the air in Gary Boyle Park. The pink-orange sky glowed behind wispy clouds in the distance, illuminating safety personnel in kayaks floating between the large inflatable buoys outlining the swim course. Ironman competitors in neon color-coded caps began lining up behind pacer athletes holding large signs printed with the times they would be finishing their swim in.

The town of Cambridge is nestled on the Chesapeake side of Maryland's Eastern shore. A welcoming town of about twelve thousand inhabitants, Cambridge was once a stop along the Underground Railroad. Bright pastel and red brick American Foursquare houses along Water Street gaze out over the

Choptank River. Peaceful suburban neighborhoods frame a small downtown area home to museums, small bistros, and a craft brewery.

Cambridge had swelled in size during the early twentieth century as a result of the Phillips Packing Company's canning operations during the World Wars, and then experienced decades of declines once the company ceased operations in the 1960s. Revitalization efforts at the turn of the millennium brought new business in the form of resorts, golf courses, and marinas. Now, wealthy yacht owners and casual boaters alike can moor their boats around the mouth of Cambridge Creek and saunter into town for modestly priced Chesapeake Bay staples like pit beef, crab cakes, and Virginia oysters.

About half a mile upriver from the Cambridge Yacht Club is Gary Boyle Park, named for the venerated Cambridge resident who had long served as the race director for the Ironman Maryland triathlon until passing in early 2019.

An Ironman triathlon is a long-distance race that consists of a 2.4-mile swim, a 112-mile bicycle ride, and a marathon run (raced back-to-back in that order). Originating in Hawaii in the late 1970s, Ironman races are now run all around the world. Twelve Ironman races occur in the United States each year, one of which is in Cambridge.

Now it was late September 2019, and the park was filled with hundreds of athletes and spectators. In the early morning twilight individuals staged their bicycles and performed their pre-race rituals. Many competitors were Ironman veterans, looking to score high enough at the Maryland race to qualify for the Ironman World Championship held every year on the island of Hawai'i. For many others, including Becca Shopiro, it was their first full-length Ironman triathlon.

Becca had grown up as a talented athlete, swimming competitively and playing water polo in high school in Illinois. She went on to play the center back position for Bucknell University's water polo team and, after graduating, continued to compete in triathlons as a way to stay physically active. "After water polo I just never wanted to give up working out in the mornings," she explained. "I always liked starting my day that way."

A lean, natural endurance athlete, Becca immediately found success in triathlon races. But it was John Zeigler, an influential water polo coach who, after running his first Ironman race for his fiftieth birthday in 2018, challenged her to complete one as well. Zeigler, who Becca had trained with at several water polo camps and had ultimately been responsible for recruiting her to Bucknell, was inspirational. With her thirtieth birthday looming on the horizon, what better goal than to complete a race that less than .001 percent of the human population has ever even attempted? In the news, the Senate Judiciary Committee hearings on Supreme Court Justice Brett Kavanaugh had just concluded, and Zeigler's challenge resonated with Becca as an opportunity to make an important statement both as a woman and as an athlete. "I was just sort of fed up with everything," she recalled.

Unlike water polo, a triathlon is an individual effort sport, requiring long hours of solitude both in training and in competition. "Every morning I would work out for one and a half hours and then I would swim twice a week," Becca described. "I would always do a long bike ride Saturday and a long run Sunday." Five- to six-hour rides are common for athletes training up for an Ironman race.

The psychological benefits of exercise have been well documented, but only within the past decade has any significant research been conducted to specifically evaluate the effects of working out alone. Thomas Plante, a professor of psychology at Santa Clara University has conducted several studies manipulating variables such as exercising indoors versus outdoors or with or without a companion. While social fitness habits hold undeniable rewards, "if your goal is to relax, reduce tension, and have a more contemplative exercise experience, then you really should consider exercising by yourself," Plante states in a *Psychology Today* blog post.[140]

Amid the mass of swimmers now gathered, Becca adjusted her bright pink racing cap and faced the starting line. In the distance, she could see the low silhouette of the Choptank River Bridge. The boom of a small cannon erupted at shoreline and a cloud of white smoke climbed above the reeds, signifying the start of the race. Racers, channelized between metal barriers, began to flow over the narrow sandy beach and into the brackish river water. Crossing under the starting archway and stepping onto the beach, Becca pulled her goggles down over her eyes.

---

140 Thomas Plante, "Your Exercise Environment Matters a Lot," *Psychology Today* (blog), February 10, 2015.

Within minutes, hundreds of bodies were splashing through the water. Swimmers dodged passing hands and feet, and everybody jockeyed for position. Becca quickly made her way around the first turn marker, making a conscious effort to quickly escape the traffic jam that inevitably occurred as racers converged on the buoy. The course consisted of two rectangular laps around the markers before returning to Gary Boyle Park.

As the first racers swam further out into the river they discovered another challenge hidden in the river: stinging sea nettles and small jellyfish that roam the Chesapeake through the summer and fall seasons. A jelly stinger brushed along skin exposed by Becca's sleeveless suit. By the time the swim ended, she would be stung two more times.

The Choptank River's current provided welcome assistance on the last long leg of the swim. Volunteers waited on the shore to help racers transition out of their neoprene wetsuits, revealing lightweight bike uniforms underneath. Once she was changed over, Becca jogged across the lot to the bicycle racks and retrieved her bike.

The 112-mile bike ride is the longest portion of an Ironman. The route snaked south out of Cambridge and into the surrounding countryside, passing the Blackwater National Wildlife Refuge before turning north back toward the city. Again, two laps were required to complete the circuit.

The first few miles came easy—Becca was in the zone. Ten miles passed, then twenty. The modest hardboard-sided houses began to spread further apart. A large high school passed by on the right-hand side of the road. Corn fields dominated the landscape as Becca sped down the cracked asphalt of the two-lane country road. Racers battled both growing fatigue and winds gusting in the wide-open areas of the racecourse. Injuries during Ironman races are commonplace, and crossing the marker for mile twenty-eight, Becca fell from her bike.

Blood flowed from a gash on her shoulder. Scrambling to her feet, Becca picked up her bike and hopped back on. Making a damage assessment while on the move, she noticed her bike's Aerobar, the cushioned pad used by racers for arm support while riding hunched forward, had collapsed and her water bottle cages were broken– meaning the infrequent aid stations spread along the course were now the only opportunities for hydration.

By lunchtime, the sun was overhead in the grey sky and Becca was cruising through Blackwater's lush forests and marshland. The Aerobar was still dangling useless between her handlebars and she was burning time stopping for water at each aid station. Endless farmland gave way, replaced by new housing developments demarcating the outskirts of Cambridge. As Becca weaved her way back through the town's narrow streets, she realized a critical error—she had missed a turn and was almost three miles off course.

Racing to double back, Becca quickly made her way to the end of the bicycle course, once again at Gary Boyle Park. Irritated by the extra five miles she had just traveled, she racked her bike and within minutes was crossing the start line for the run. She had 26.2 miles left.

Nearly eight hours into the Ironman and beginning the final leg, Becca recalled her frustration: "I was so mad that when I went to run I was holding a 7:00 to 8:20 minute pace for the first six miles… and then I just tanked."

Although her pace dropped, she dug deep and pressed on, maintaining an even pace. "It's just grueling, ya know?" Becca said, reflecting on the experience. "You go to very dark places in your mind sometimes." Eleven hours, twenty-nine minutes, and fifteen seconds after stepping into the water at the start line, Becca grinned as she jogged across the finish. The sun was beginning to set, and the sky was once again a warm pastel. Despite being her first Ironman race (also the first full marathon she had ever run), Becca finished in the top 5 percent of female athletes.

For Ironman athletes, physical endurance must be accompanied by deep-rooted mental resiliency. In 2012, Kayla Frimmel presented research to the Department of Health Sciences and Kinesiology at Georgia Southern University entitled "Mental Preparation Techniques and Accomplishment of Race Goals by Ironman Triathletes: A Qualitative Investigation."

In the study, Frimmel cited "choice of focus" as one of the driving factors for Ironman athletes, stating "while they focused on a variety of things at various times, the commonality was having control of the focus and knowing where to direct it." Specifically focusing on self-talk as a motivational technique, the researchers listed themes that athletes directed their mind toward, including self-confidence, control and mental readiness, and relaxation (imagine that).[141]

Focusing on physical tasks creates a presence that can be otherwise difficult to attain in everyday life. For Becca, developing such a focus is a holistic practice that permeates multiple aspects of life, extending beyond athletic competition and into artistic outlets. In Washington, DC, right on Georgetown's bustling M Street and a short walk from major tourist attractions like the Waterfront Park and Georgetown Cupcake, you will find REWILD, a local plant and flower studio. Inside, among waxy succulents and hanging baskets with philodendrons cascading out of them, you can find pottery that Becca sculpts in a nearby studio.

A practice started in high school, rediscovered in college, and sustained for years after, Becca's work can now be found in stores around DC. "I picked it back up as a way to have detox time in college," Becca explained. "It really is a centering practice because you have to center the clay on the wheel and it takes all of your concentration and focus to put your energy into making the clay centered."

"Throwing pottery" is the process of shaping a piece of clay on a spinning wheel. The clay must be centered in order for a potter to be able to then mold it by hand as the wheel spins rapidly. "Sometimes it's really hard to center the clay and it's wobbly and it sort of reflects a feeling of instability," Becca

---

141 Kayla Frimmel, "Mental Preparation Techniques and Accomplishments of Race Goals by Ironman Triathletes: A Qualitative Investigation" (master's thesis, Georgia Southern University, 2012), 36.

says. "Keeping it centered as you're shaping the object feels like a meditative sort of practice."

The time Becca spends unplugged, clocking miles in the pool or sitting in front of a spinning lump of clay, helps put her into that "zone" or default mode where the mind can do its deep thinking. The brain's default mode is not just a brightly colored computer screensaver floating aimlessly behind our eyes. In a 2015 paper, researchers from Cornell, Harvard, and York Universities describe how "constructing future simulations is closely associated with default network activity, as details of personal episodic events are recombined into an imagined future."[142]

In layman's terms, this is "autobiographical planning." Manoush Zomorodi describes it in her TED Talk on boredom and creativity: "This is when we look back at our lives, we take note of the big moments, we create a personal narrative, and then we set goals and we figure out what steps we need to take to reach them."[143]

"When I work out in the morning, that's when I have a lot of my ideas for work," Becca says. "Or even just if I'm trying to solve a problem, or there was an argument... I'm more conscious of my thought process."

She then carries that creative mindset with her as she leaves the gym and heads to her office at the Center on Poverty and

---

142 R. Nathan Spreng et al., "Autobiographical planning and the brain: Activation and its modulation by qualitative features," *Journal of Cognitive Neuroscience*, 27, no. 11 (2015): 2147-57.

143 *Ted* "How boredom can lead to your most brilliant ideas | Manoush Zomorodi," August 29, 2017, video, 16:13.

Inequality at Georgetown Law, where her team's mandate is "to support low-income girls and girls of color by identifying barriers to girls' health and wellbeing, elevating girls' unique assets and needs, and developing policy and programs to better support girls in our public systems."[144]

Becca points out that the ability to pursue creative outlets is not equally shared by all. "I think mindfulness has helped my ability at work to recognize privilege, to seek opportunities to learn and grow, and to learn how to be comfortable outside of my comfort zone," she says. "We need that in this world, now more than ever—to learn how to be quiet, to listen to other peoples' experiences, and to question our own conditioning and biases."

For Becca, stepping up to the challenge of an Ironman was an important statement "as a woman who was turning thirty and graduating business school and feeling sort of lost." Centering practices through exercise and creative outlets are lifelong skills she uses to be mindful of herself and others. Being able to escape, even for brief periods of time, allows her to return to her work energized. "I had grown such a positive relationship with working out and with creating artwork as a means to create time for myself," she explains, "so rather than feeling lost and feeling like there were things that were out of my control that I wasn't happy with, I learned to turn to pottery and working out and this extreme sense of just being in the zone for so long as a way to feel centered again, you know?"

---

144 "The Center on Poverty and Inequality," Georgetown Law, accessed September 16, 2020.

## CAN PHYSICAL FITNESS MAKE US KINDER TO OTHERS?

The links between physical activity and mental performance have been extensively studied, but what exactly is the link between fitness and kindness (social performance, if you will)? Let's begin with the connection between anxiety and empathy. A 2017 study published by Cambridge University Press found that anxiety widens an "empathy gap" already existing between our "ingroup" (i.e., the people in your close circles) and our "outgroup" (i.e., everyone else).[145] In plain terms, as our anxiety increases, our willingness to empathize with those outside of our immediate relationships decreases.

How can fitness counter this effect? By reducing our anxiety levels. A letter to the editor in *The Primary Care Companion to the Journal of Clinical Psychiatry* sheds some light by explaining that aerobic exercise, including "jogging, swimming, cycling, walking, gardening, and dancing, have been proved to reduce anxiety and depression."[146] The meta-analysis they cite prescribes routines that are:[147]

- Fifteen to thirty minutes in duration
- Performed a minimum of three times a week
- Part of a larger program of ten-week weeks or longer

145 Kevin Arceneaux, "Anxiety Reduces Empathy Toward Outgroup Members But Not Ingroup Members," *Journal of Experimental Political Science*, 4, no. 1, (Spring 2017): 68-80.

146 Monika Guszkowska, "Effects of exercise on anxiety, depression and mood [in Polish]," *Psychiatria Polska*, 38 (2004): 611–620., as cited in Ashish Sharma, Vishal Madaan, and Frederick D. Petty, "Exercise for Mental Health," *The Primary Care Companion to the Journal of Clinical Psychiatry*, 8, no. 2 (2006): 106.

147 Monika Guszkowska, "Effects of exercise on anxiety, depression and mood [in Polish]," *Psychiatria Polska*, 38 (2004): 611–620.

A pretty low bar for some serious mental health benefits. You can undoubtedly carve fifteen minutes out a few times a week to get some fresh air and perspective, even if it just means pushing a stroller around the block or walking the dog. Could hitting the pool or the pavement and throwing the brain into its default mode make us more considerate of others as well as ourselves? More research is required to definitively link fitness to our affective and cognitive empathy. However, next time you find yourself wrestling with how to feel about an uncomfortable interaction or thought, step away from the problem for a few minutes and find a physical task to focus on. As those endorphins pump through your body, you will be pleasantly surprised by the perspective you can discover.

# COLLECTIVE

———

*"Having been profoundly shocked by the revelation that my wartime experiences were haunting me without my conscious knowledge, I made the very difficult decision to try to consciously remember what had happened and to write it all down as a form of therapy."*

—NICHOLAS WARR, PHASE LINE GREEN

Norton Juster, the aforementioned author of the *The Phantom Tollbooth*, first began writing to combat boredom while serving in the US Navy. He has lived an interesting and eclectic life characterized by mischievous creativity, inventing fun where none was to be found. At one point, he founded a club he called the Garibaldi Society, the sole purpose of which was to reject all applications for membership. Most importantly though, he has gifted the world with entertaining and fantastical children's literature that inspires to this day. After all, one of the best uses for the creative mind is to find creative ways to give back to the world.

Two such innovative minds, Keith Dow and Tyler Carroll, met in the US Army in 2012 while they were stationed in Vicenza, Italy. Situated south of the Dolomites and in between Milan and Venice, Vicenza is a cosmopolitan gem where piazze sit in the shade of iconic Palladian architecture. It is the birthplace of Luigi Da Porto, the Italian writer most widely known for his novella *Giulietta e Romeo*, which would later become the source material for Shakespeare's famous tragedy, *Romeo and Juliet*.

Vicenza is also the location of a United States Army garrison home to thousands of American soldiers, civilians, military retirees and families. There, a close friendship developed between Dow and Carroll.

Dow was from the rocky North Shore between Boston and New Hampshire. Growing up influenced by heavy hardcore bands like Terror and Death Before Dishonor, Dow spent his post-high school years bouncing around in New England's hardcore music scene, working casual jobs, and touring the northeast with a friend's band. In 2008 he had taken a break from life on the road and was working two jobs, one of which was at a college bar, where he became captivated by the stories of recently returned veterans of the Global War on Terror. Hungry for adventure and camaraderie, Dow enlisted and became a military policeman. By the time he and Carroll met in 2012, he had already completed assignments in Washington and Iraq and was planning to get out of the army the following year.

Tyler Carroll grew up in a military family and, at nineteen years old, after a brief pass at college, decided that he would join the army instead. Carroll became a combat medic and was assigned to the 173rd Airborne Brigade, a decorated unit whose troops were nicknamed the "Sky Soldiers." The 173rd was headquartered in Vicenza. When Carroll arrived, the brigade was working up for a deployment to Afghanistan—its fourth Afghan deployment in a span of six years.

On June 14, 2012, the 173rd gathered on the sunny parade grounds of Caserma Ederle and ceremoniously cased its colors—a practice deeply rooted in American military tradition where a unit places its flags into storage prior to deploying. Within a month, the 173rd was engaged in heavy fighting with insurgents across Logar and Wardak provinces. The 173rd set up its command post at Forward Operating Base Shank, in Logar. Logar province was predominantly occupied by ethnic Pashtuns belonging to Ghilzai tribal confederation, a tribe historically known for its warrior culture. Much of the Taliban's leadership, including its infamous founder, Mullah Muhammed Omar, were Ghilzai.

Due to Logar's tribal dynamics and its role as a strategic gateway to Kabul, the province was a frequent hotbed of Taliban and insurgent activity. FOB Shank, located just south of Logar's capital, Puli Alam, earned the nickname "Rocket City" from the near constant barrage of rocket and mortar shells that rained down from the surrounding countryside.

Carroll's unit, D Company, 1st Battalion, 503rd Infantry Regiment, was located at Combat Outpost (COP) Kherwar, nestled along the western edge of the Spīn Ghar mountain range, an hour south of FOB Shank near the village of Bakshikhala. The rocky, barren ground was dotted with occasional fields of wheat, vegetable, and forage crops. High-walled mud compounds were scattered between the fields and surrounding hillsides, which the Taliban used to launch regular attacks on the COP.

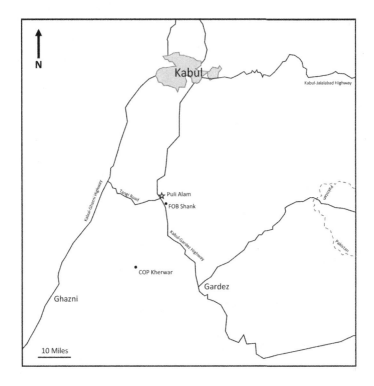

On July 27, COP Kherwar came under attack from small arms fire. Incoming bullets slapped into the COP's HESCO barrier fortifications, kicking up dust and clods of dirt. Return fire thundered from machine gun positions as paratroopers called out enemy positions in the hills. Orange tracer rounds zipped over the battlefield, occasionally ricocheting off of the ground and into the sky before burning out and disappearing. Another flurry of incoming fire struck a soldier near Carroll. Pinned down, Carroll and several others dragged the wounded man to cover in a nearby CONEX box, a thin-skinned metal shipping container converted for expeditionary storage. Carroll and another soldier, twenty-three-year-old Private First Class Theo Glende, attended to the wounded man, performing essential combat lifesaving. With the soldiers now stationary, the Taliban began to fire mortars at the compound. As the shells struck all over COP Kherwar, Glende and Carroll were wounded—Glende, a bright kid from Rochester, New York, with an "encyclopedic-like brain," fatally so.[148]

"One of the most lonely times in my life and where I felt I got the most personal growth and what's really shaped me today was when I got hurt in Afghanistan and the recovery afterward," Carroll recalled when we spoke, "because it wasn't just a physical battle, it was a mental battle."

Carroll was sent home to Texas to recover from his wounds. The recovery proved to be a spiritual journey as much as a physical one. "My whole sole purpose in the military was to become deemed fit for duty. I was doing physical therapy five days a week, plus trying to work out on my own, and so I had this outlet, which was the gym. But that's only a couple hours a day." The rest of the time, Carroll found himself dependent on the help of his family.

"To humble yourself to ask for that help is extremely important," Carroll said, "but at the same time, not rely on them and find creative ways to take care of yourself."

---

148  Kent Harris, "Four soldiers honored at Vicenza memorial service," *Stars and Stripes*, August 2, 2012.

"That whole journey, it was a lot of just on my own trying to figure out where do I want to go from this? Do I want to just say, 'Alright, that just happened and I'm done,' or do I want to be better? And I decided I want to be better." Between physical therapy and workouts, Carroll dove into books, particularly the bible. In the midst of this recovery, Carroll also discovered another outlet: writing.

Veterans are pervasive throughout the world of literature: Thirty-three years before *The Lion, The Witch, and The Wardrobe* was published, C.S. Lewis was fighting in the trenches of the Somme. J.R.R. Tolkien had served in the same trenches two years prior. George Orwell fought against fascist forces and was wounded by a sniper during the Spanish Civil War. Royal Air Force pilot Roald Dahl flew Hurricane fighters in combat in World War II two decades before he wrote *James and the Giant Peach* and *Charlie and the Chocolate Factory.*

Carroll filled his spare time with writing short essays and poetry. He found the creative process provided focus and clarity, aiding his recovery. "Training in the gym was initially kind of where it started, and then with reading, and then with writing, was the progression" Carroll described. "I was able to just focus in on one thing, and I had to teach myself how to do it."

Even today, Carroll cannot be found without a notepad. "Now writing, I'm able to think so much clearer at the end of it because I'm focusing on just one specific topic, one specific idea, one specific emotion, one specific event, whatever the case may be, and really dissect how I feel and think about something. And that writing has helped me out tremendously as far as processing that information."

While Carroll recovered and rejoined his unit, he and Keith Dow kept in touch. Dow, now married and living in Ontario where he was a student at Georgian College, had not forgotten his comrades in arms. He helped organize events to support the veteran community, including a seven-day, three-hundred-kilometer (186-mile) ruck march that raised money to build a retreat in Northern Ontario for veterans and first responders struggling with post-traumatic stress.

Dow was deeply impacted by his time in the army, and he was keenly aware of the toll that America's longest running conflict was taking on the veteran community. He zeroed in on a problem he perceived as the roughhewn and ephemeral nature of the GWOT generation's thoughts and stories—at the time, mostly relegated to posts on social media. "What a waste this shit is," Dow, not one to mince words, observed. "What a waste social media is for somebody to pour their soul into a status. And eventually, you know, if you've been around long enough to know what MySpace and Friendster were, eventually it's just going to go away."

The modern military in the age of social media is at risk of losing the ability to enshrine its thoughts and memories in a meaningful way that can inform future generations. "You know, the website is going to crash, or something else is going to come along, but either way, those words are lost," Dow says. The solution was apparent to him: encourage the veteran community to *create* again. "Something where these rants without punctuation, or spacing, or any kind of full sculpting that a written piece should, can have some finishing and it can have a little bit of class but the point can still be delivered."

Dow started reaching out to veterans about starting a blog, Black Coffee Response—a name that eventually changed to the Dead Reckoning Collective to differentiate the blog from Black Rifle Coffee Company, an unrelated veteran-owned coffee company that took off around the same time. At the time, Dow was completely unaware that Carroll had been writing.

Carroll had made a full physical recovery and returned to duty with his unit back in Italy. His initial contract was nearing its end, and he was looking for what would become the next chapter in life.

In 2015, while he was deployed to Turkey to support Operation Active Fence, the United States' contribution to the NATO Patriot missile defense mission, a friend mentioned the fire service and Carroll instantly knew that was the answer. It was an opportunity to return to his community and continue serving and helping others.

When Carroll saw posts from Dow online seeking out veteran writers, he sent a message asking for feedback on a piece written about his injury. "As soon as I looked at it, I made some edits, but I knew it was gonna be the first piece that we released," Dow said. The two formed a partnership and began making plans to expand the Dead Reckoning Collective. "Instead of just a blog where people could share stories on the internet we wanted to actually put out books" Dow explained. "We wanted to help facilitate creative projects."

Carroll agreed with Dow's assessment of the need to give veteran creatives a voice, especially because expressing pain was such a thematic and difficult subject for so many people to broach. "How sad is it that people like themselves so little that they have to escape themselves?" Carroll lamented. "Everybody was trying to distract themselves so much and at the same time nobody was interacting with anybody." He knew from experience that taking time for inner focus and expression was essential to healing, but it was not the end of the journey.

"You're in this solitude for so long. But what really confirms that self-growth is displaying it to the world, displaying it to your friends, your family, and them liking that transformation," Carroll says. "It's good to create on your own, whether that's drawing, writing or anything, but when other people talk about it, it shows that you're saying something that needs to be said, or thinking something, or writing something that needs to be said or heard."

Dead Reckoning Collective is a name filled with meaning. Dead reckoning is one of the oldest and simplest methods of navigation. By understanding one's starting location, direction, and distance of travel, one can navigate from one point to another. Christopher Columbus and John Cabot crossed the Atlantic using dead reckoning. It is still taught in the military and remains a staple for special operations selection (reference the earlier chapter on navigating through the woods).

DEAD RECKONING
20 17
COLLECTIVE

Carroll, who passed selection for Army Special Forces (i.e., the Green Berets) found that land navigation was a unique challenge. "It wasn't necessarily because plotting points and finding them was hard, but you're by yourself for twelve hours, hating life, questioning why you're doing this the whole time" he says. "And so you got to have kind of a why and a reason in order to get through that." For the Dead Reckoning Collective, the raison d'être is helping to navigate the challenges of life for many in the veteran community. The "Collective" portion of the name reflects that even if many veterans are creating on their own, there is a gathering place and community that still encourages them to share.

The first major project published by the newly formed Dead Reckoning Collective came in January of 2019 in the form of a collection of over fifty poems written by Dow and Carroll entitled *Fact and Memory.*

"To be honest, the first book was a test run," Dow explained in an interview with *Coffee or Die* magazine (ironically enough, the web magazine for the Black Rifle Coffee Company). "Tyler and I knew the kind of things we wanted to publish, but this was the first chance for us to work together on something with our own writing. We wanted to get the [publishing] process down and make any mistakes with our own material before screwing it up for someone else's work."[149]

Two months later the Dead Reckoning Collective published *In Love... &War: The Anthology of Poet Warriors,* a collaboration with Leo Jenkins, another prolific GWOT poet, which includes poetry from thirty-eight veterans.

From the Collective's bootstrapping origins, Dow and Carroll have grown it into a brand that is the de facto meeting place for veteran artists of all types. The pair have hosted more than two dozen podcast episodes where they interview veterans from all walks of life. They have run social media campaigns encouraging veterans to create more. And if that sounds dissonant from Dow's original complaint about posting on social media, it helps to know that all of the campaigns push people to create things that exist outside of the digital world. They have run several thirty-day "hand-written

---

149 Tim Cooper, "A Fresh Voice in the Veteran Community? Meet Dead Reckoning Collective," *Coffee or Die Magazine,* May 6, 2019.

challenges" where they provide a writing prompt and people share photos of their responses written out on a scrap of notebook paper, rather than tap-typed onto the touchscreen of a cell phone.

The founders of Dead Reckoning Collective: Keith Dow (left) and Tyler Carroll (right).

A 2017 study on the role of an individual's internal and external resources in contributing to physical and psychological quality of life discovered that "people with greater levels of self-efficacy and resilience can mobilize emotional and psychological resources to face the stressful elements of their lives, and therefore, to express and feel more [Quality of Life] satisfaction." The study defines the concept of self-efficacy as "a perspective that considers people as having an active role in producing and giving meaning to their experiences."[150]

From the beginning, life involves personal struggle of some type. While the human experience varies greatly, what is important is reflecting on those experiences that we go through as individuals and using them as creative fuel not only for ourselves but for our community. We can use our unique perspectives and experiences to elevate the self-efficacy and resilience of the people around us, just as Dow and Carroll are doing by connecting veterans.

"Tyler and I would like to call ourselves social entrepreneurs," Dow says. "There's definitely not just this capitalist agenda that we have. We're constantly trying to leave the world better than we found it with what we're doing." Despite now living more than 1,500 miles apart, Keith Dow and Tyler Carroll remain closer than ever. Keith lives with his wife and two children just north of the Greater Toronto Area and is completing his graduate studies at the Master of Social Work program at the University of New England. Tyler has been a part of the fire service in Flower Mound, Texas, for four years. He and his wife are raising three young children—a daughter and two sons, one of whom is named Theo.

150  Eva Gerino et al., "Loneliness, Resilience, Mental Health, and Quality of Life in Old Age: A Structural Equation Model," *Frontiers in Psychology*, no. 8 (November 2017): 2003.

# MONOMYTH

---

*"Seek to make your life long and its purpose in the service of your people."*

— *TECUMSEH*

In 1932, Joseph Campbell was living in a modest cottage perched above the small town of Pacific Grove in Monterey County, California. Much of his time was spent with his friends, biologist and philosopher Ed Ricketts (who was his neighbor) and writer John Steinbeck.[151] There, in Campbell's "Canary Cottage" home, he scrawled into his journal: "Intelligent criticism of contemporary values ought to be useful to the world. This gets back again to Krishna's dictum: 'The best way to help mankind is through the perfection of yourself.'"[152]

Campbell is best known for his exploration of the philosophy of heroes and mythology. George Lucas later credited

---

151 "Joseph Campbell Gets a Tree in Carmel-by-the-Sea," *Pacific Graduate Institute Alumni Association* (blog), May 2, 2018, accessed 14 September 2020.

152 "Joseph Campbell," *Esalen*, accessed 14 September 2020.

Campbell's work for having a direct influence on the plots of the original Star Wars movies.[153] Campbell spent his life building a reputation as an authority on the literature of heroes. Perhaps one of his greater contributions was his work *The Hero with a Thousand Faces*, published in 1949.

In it, he explores the common narrative themes and archetypes found in mythology and folklore tales. He outlines his take on the Hero's Journey, a ubiquitous template that describes a story's hero who departs on an adventure, confronts and overcomes an existential challenge, and returns transformed. Campbell, a voracious reader of comparative religious texts, outlined the basic stages of a mythic cycle, exploring common variations in the Hero's Journey, which, he argues, is a metaphor for both an individual and an entire a culture. He cites Gautama Buddha's journey as fitting the Hero's Journey archetype.[154]

Each of the stories enclosed in *The Lonesome Thread* has an epilogue. Andy Puddicombe's journey of self-discovery ultimately is what led him to the creation of Headspace, which touches millions of lives every day. The "Chosin Few" Marines' escape to the sea allowed them to provide critical reinforcement to other battlefronts, ensuring that South Korea was preserved as a free nation. John "Red" Parkinson, who held his dying friend in his arms and spent

153 Lucas Seastrom, "Mythic Discovery Within the Inner Reaches of Outer Space: Joseph Campbell Meets George Lucas - Part I," October 22, 2015, accessed 14 September 2020.

154 Joseph Campbell, *The Hero with a Thousand Faces*, (California: New World Library, 2008), 25-31.

decades after the Korean War plagued with post-traumatic stress disorder, eventually sought treatment and then used the tools he learned to help other veterans through their struggles.

Jim Stockdale, barely able to walk when he returned to the United States, became a modern thought leader in Stoic philosophy. His wife Sybil helped to found the League of American Families of POWs and MIAs, which she also served as its first chairman. Ignatius of Loyola's crippling wounds altered his warrior's path, leading him instead to a life in the service of others.

Becca Shopiro's daily retreats in the gym and in front of a pottery wheel allow her to approach her job, helping underprivileged girls of color, with a clear and compassionate mind. Keith Dow and Tyler Carroll's journeys in search of post-war meaning have led them to become better husbands, fathers, and friends, inspiring them to encourage other veterans to do the same.

A 2005 study published in the *International Journal of Behavioral Medicine* demonstrates that a strong correlation exists between the well-being, happiness, health, and longevity of emotionally and behaviorally compassionate people.[155] In a more recent study, researchers from Columbia University and MIT discovered that people who are eager to help others regulate their emotions (i.e., putting the needs of others before their own emotional needs) "showed greater decreases

---

155 Steven G. Post, "Altruism, happiness, and health: it's good to be good," *International Journal of Behavioral Medicine*, 12, (2005): 66-77.

in depression, mediated by increased use of reappraisal in daily life."[156]

The lives we build for ourselves allow us to do amazing things. Millennials often lament coming-of-age in the midst a jobless recovery and losing the opportunity to build wealth in the same ways that the preceding generations have. Many in Generation Z are also finding themselves hamstrung out of the gates by a dearth of career opportunities in the wake of the COVID-19 health crisis. Despite this, these generations hold the keys to future happiness: time.

The time we spend exploring our inner life and realizing our true self produces a dividend that is paid out to the community—value that we generate and share with the people in our lives. The 2012 World Happiness Report, produced by the United Nations Sustainable Development Solutions Network, points out that after our basic needs are met, a healthy social life correlates highly with our happiness. Income matters up to a certain degree, but once basic needs are met the report highlights the fact that cooperation and community are some of the largest contributors to happiness in wealthy societies.[157]

In his book *The Algebra of Happiness*, serial entrepreneur and NYU professor Scott Galloway writes that being excited to see someone you care about "focuses you on your better

156  Bruce P. Doré, "Helping Others Regulate Emotion Predicts Increased Regulation of One's Own Emotions and Decreased Symptoms of Depression," *Personality and Social Psychology Bulletin*, 43, no. 5 (2017): 729-739.

157  Helliwell, Layard, and Sachs, ed., "World Happiness Report," *The Earth Institute*, (Commissioned for the United Nations Conference on Happiness, New York, NY, April 2, 2012), 7-8.

self, the self who cares about others."[158] If happiness through social engagement seems antithetical to the thesis of this book, consider that by striking a balance in our schedule and focusing on ourselves we can offer more to the community. Solitude does not have to be a selfish endeavor. Instead, treat it as a tool to become a better steward of our community's mental health. Any book you have ever read—including this one—would not have been created and shared with the world were it not for someone spending long periods with their head down and a pen in their hand.

It is important to view life as a series of adventures that build upon one another, but also to realize that the ultimate payoff is a wiser and more grounded return to society at the end. Friar Richard Rohr builds upon Carl Jung's concept of "the two halves of life" in his book *Falling Upward*. The adventures of the first half establish our sense of self identity, what Freud calls the "ego self." "But inevitably you discover, often through failure or a significant loss, that your conscious self is not all of you, but only the acceptable you," Rohr explains in a blog post for the Center for Action and Contemplation, which he founded. "You will find your real purpose and identity at a much deeper level than the positive image you present to the world."[159]

Six days before finishing the Individual Training Course, the nine-month initial training for Marine Corps special operations, I found out I would not be graduating. A few

---

158  Scott Galloway, *The Algebra of Happiness: Notes on the Pursuit of Success, Love, and Meaning*, (New York: Portfolio, 2019), 180.

159  Richard Rohr, "The Two Halves of Life," *Daily Meditations* (blog), *Center for Action and Contemplation*, October 12, 2015.

weeks later, my wife and I, emotionally exhausted, made the decision to separate. Between special operations training in North Carolina and her attending law school in California, we had seen each other less than seven days over the past year.

Instead of realizing dreams of leading special operations commandos on missions around the world, I was reassigned to a small training unit, responsible for preparing other units for deployment overseas, where I worked alone for a majority of my time. My service obligation to the Marine Corps meant I had to remain in North Carolina for an additional two years, most of which were spent living alone in a house with my dog Bailey. The coastal region of southeastern North Carolina is sparsely populated, and living near Marine Corps Base Camp Lejeune meant living isolated from the rest of civilization.

At that time, stripped of all of the things that, up to that point in my life, had given me both professional and personal meaning, I found myself in a perilous struggle of self-identity. Additionally, working in solitude meant I had an unprecedented amount of unstructured time. Sitting alone with my dog as hours, days, weeks, and months silently crept by, I finally crawled from this low point and began to ascribe new meaning to the losses I had encountered.

I am a privileged person. There are far worse lots in life than the conditions I found myself in. But shattering the illusions of identity I had built for myself allowed me to wrestle with the existential issues many people struggle with on a daily basis. While I still on occasion wistfully think of the future I had *originally* envisioned, I have walked a new path that has yielded its own reward, far in excess of my own imagination.

Lisa Directo-Davis points out that many young professionals are groomed to think of themselves on a constant upward trajectory, and that upon experiencing a massive setback, "you think 'my life will be a disaster.'" In this mindset, she explains, "The imagination of what can be good becomes so narrow." My stumbling stone was an opportunity to create and explore new ideas and, through doing so, build a healthy inner-life. As Directo-Davis describes, when we build a mindful and introspective practice we are "not a new person, but a remembering of ourselves as our truest self."

Leaving the military and rejoining society, as it is for many veterans, felt like I was stepping off of a UFO and seeing earth for the first time. Since then, I have loved, lost, argued, learned, and generally tried to reintegrate about as successfully as the next guy. I've had setbacks, and will have more, but I try to approach each day with gratitude and humility, knowing I am a wiser person than I was the day before—a perspective only made possible by first being cast out of my previous identities.

***

**KILIMANJARO: A LESSON IN FINDING INNER STRENGTH FOR THOSE AROUND YOU**
At some point just after midnight on one of the first days of 2020, I found myself clinging to the side of Mount

Kilimanjaro, Africa's tallest summit. We had started in the pitch black of night at an elevation of around 15,300 feet. With me were nine other climbers, mostly Georgetown MBA students like myself. Despite gradually conditioning our bodies over the previous week, the low air pressure starved our muscles of oxygen and hypoxia quickly set in. Every step became a struggle, and walking even a short distance left us bent over, nauseous and gasping for air.

An unseasonable storm had blown in the day before and now it pounded down on top of us. A sustained seventy-mile-per-hour wind picked up dirt, rock, and ice and whipped it into a maelstrom that punished us from every direction, freezing and stinging every centimeter of exposed skin around our hands and faces. At each break our group huddled together, holding each other to keep from blowing off of the jagged rocks and into what felt like an infinite void of darkness. The volcanic mountainside blended into the storm clouds, offering no discernible demarcation from where the steep trail ended and a long fall began.

Gusts of jet-stream-level wind inflated the pack cover of the woman in front of me, and I considered that it looked very much like a parachute slider, flapping in the wind. No sooner had this thought materialized than another gust ripped the pack cover completely off. In another instant, it was gone forever. The only thing keeping me grounded in the darkness was the gravity of our small team's situation. As I squinted into the darkness at the faces of my friends, I witnessed internal struggle of an unprecedented nature.

I flashed back to a cornfield in Helmand Province Afghanistan, dimly lit in steel-blue nautical twilight. I saw our patrol, drenched in sweat and exhausted, redistributing heavy gear so that no Marine fell behind as we raced the sunset to our pickup point. Another gust of icy wind snapped me back to the present moment. The familiar feeling of being "in the shit" gave me the confidence to help navigate the uninitiated. I made a commitment to leave no teammate alone on the mountain. I watched as the stronger climbers gripped the hands of the others and pulled them up the mountainside to the summit, refusing to give up on the team.

The psychological summits we climb help us to guide the people we encounter in life that are standing at the base of their own mountains, staring up at the imposing peaks. We reached Stella Point—a notch at the top of our long climb, just as the sun cracked open the countryside behind us. Long orange rays spilled across the valley below, illuminating ashen clouds and alpine desert miles below us. I followed the last of our team to a flat area, and we spun to face the sunrise. We gasped for breath as we sucked in the thin mountain air. I considered that this would not have felt like an accomplishment were it not for the people I climbed alongside. The silent confidence that comes from deep knowledge of self creates the most happiness for us when we are using it in the service of others.

Sunrise at Stella Point.

\*\*\*

Living and reliving the Hero's Journey establishes our important first-half-of-life self. By embracing moments of solitude, retreat, and withdrawal, we can unlock our creative minds and use what we find there to rejoin the world as better members of society, fully prepared to give back to those in our lives. Once we have done the deep-down work and built a healthy inner life, we can live more complete outer lives as well. As Rohr describes it in *Falling Upward*, "Quite simply, my desire and effort—every day—is to pay back, to give back to the world a bit of what I have received."[160] Do

---

160  Richard Rohr, *Falling Upward: A Spirituality for the Two Halves of Life*, (San Francisco: Jossey-Bass, 2011), 121.

not run from those in-between moments of boredom and loneliness—use them as opportunities to discover the wonders of inner life. All of humankind will be better off for it.

# PRIVILEGE
# (AN EPILOGUE)

---

*"Why, sometimes I've believed as many as six impossible things before breakfast."*

—*THE RED QUEEN,* THROUGH THE LOOKING-
GLASS *BY LEWIS CARROLL*

The table has just been cleared. I can hear Dad one room over rinsing dishes from the dinner he made. We have just finished one of his famous meals—the opulent sort that neighbors and relatives talk about for weeks and for him is another epicurean experiment that materialized in his mind as effortlessly as tying a pair of shoes.

I am sitting at the end of the table, listening to Mom regale my girlfriend with a story about Halloween costumes. My mother, an energetic bootstrapper, hand-made costumes for my brother and I every year growing up. Having learned to sew and craft as a function of theatrical costume design, her creations were a labor of love for both self-expression and for her children. A French Pierrot one year, a hand-painted velociraptor formed out of foam, a gigantic human head—if we could imagine it, she could make it. I have heard these same stories a thousand times, but a smile creases under my eyes as I hear them for the thousand-and-first. A memory of a child barely present in my own consciousness but one that is vivid in the memory of both of my parents.

The lens I view the world through comes from having two parents who sacrificed immeasurably in order to give two boys a weltanschauung where we were only limited by imagination.

I learned to swim because my mother—who never learned growing up—decided it was a requirement for her kids. I absorbed adventure and history novels because my father filled our house with beautifully written and designed books. Even if we did not have much, I had it good because of them, and that has made all the difference.

Midway through 2020, on a different trip up to my childhood home in Frederick, Maryland, I made an offhand remark to my mother that I was working on a book. The subject matter was very much the product of an upbringing that emphasized an appreciation for the arts combined with a nontraditional path that I blazed for myself in the military. She was quick to offer her thoughts on my connection of boredom and creativity:

"I am *never* bored," she proclaimed. We were late into the night and deep into a bottle of Italian white. "Being bored means you're stuck—and I refuse to be... I refuse to be bored."

"There are plenty of people who are probably bored," I countered, "but have no choice but to be. Like if they're stuck in a meeting—I think a lot of people don't have the financial freedom or time to pursue their goals. It comes from a place of privilege to be able to do that."

Writing a book is no small undertaking, even for someone who loves to write. I could not help but think of the talented people whose lives do not offer them an outlet for their creative sides. What about all of the sleep-deprived parents who barely have ten minutes to take a shower in solitude, much less meditate in their kitchen? Where is the book for all of the kids who can barely afford a school lunch, let alone a college education? The Marine Corps had been my ticket to both an education and a career, but what about the many for whom military service was out of reach? Sheepishly, I considered that it in any other circumstances, writing a book about creative solitude was at best impossible, and at worst ostentatious.

"But there are plenty of examples of people who were poor or underprivileged who can overcome their obstacles," she pointed out. "If there's a will, there's a way."

"You wouldn't be able to travel the world fencing if you had two small children. It just logistically would not be feasible," I replied.

"Well, there will be sacrifices," Mom, rarely one to concede in a debate, admitted. "For me when you guys were little, you were everything. Once you got to a certain point, it's like, 'Okay these guys can do stuff on their own. They don't need me as much. I can do stuff for myself.' I had to—you guys are only little for so long."

Thus, I realized an important observation: Some people just are not at a place in their lives where they have the amount of freedom to pursue all of the things they envision for themselves in their minds' eye. The distinction is that one can never lose focus on their own deep-down character and interests through it all. Think of the Stockdale Paradox—meet every circumstance head on but never once question yourself or that you will prevail. When Fortuna turns her rudder and our boat begins to tack in a different direction, we must remember that our course still carries us forward. How we comport ourselves in troubled waters determines how seaworthy the vessel of our life is.

"When it comes down to making those sacrifices, it's all about knowing yourself and what is important to you." My mother did not need to read my book to understand the message I wanted to convey to the world.

This book contains stories and messages that are important to me because of the life I have lived. It has a flavor unique to the way I walk the world, and I will be the first to acknowledge that many opportunities I have been afforded only as a result of the sacrifices of people who loved me unconditionally.

Throughout the process of writing this book, the world has borne witness to unprecedented crises that have held a mirror up to our societies and questioned the validity of everything that came before 2020. From how we conduct business to how we treat others, a long-overdue examination is underway, and inshallah the world will come out a better place in the long run. I wrote *The Lonesome Thread* because life is too short to mince words about what we want for ourselves, and the most noble thing to want is a better world for those around us. The discoveries we make as we pull our own lonesome threads only matter if they are made for the sake of the rest of humanity.

# APPENDIX A: COMPASS

---

*"Bottom line: Be certain of your position. Do not simply talk yourself into it!"*

—BASIC OFFICER COURSE B182036, MILITARY

TOPOGRAPHIC MAP II, STUDENT HANDOUT, C. 2011

Despite the Marine Corps' Basic Officer Course (colloquially "The Basic School," "The Big Suck," "Thousands Being Stupid," "The Bummer Summer," or just plain-old TBS) being considered merely entry-level training, it offers some of the best (and most challenging) land navigation instruction a young second lieutenant can get his or her tender, uncalloused hands on. As a wide-eyed boot officer, you either "get it" or you spend your weekends wandering Quantico's hilly forests conducting remedial training until you do.

In researching and writing the initial chapters of this book, I was inspired to revisit some of the TBS student handouts and peruse the land navigation sections. I will spare you from the cryptic publication references, Enabling and Terminal Learning Objectives, and general pedagogy of orienteering land navigation, but thought it would be a fun and useful exercise to include a down-and-dirty recounting of some best practices I have found over the course of almost eight years of being professionally lost in the woods.

Three things you will need:

- Orientation (Origin and Destination)
- Direction (Compass)
- Distance (Pace count)

Let's start with an origin point and a destination. Topographic map reading, while generally pretty intuitive, is worth explaining here. The most important concept is to associate the lines you are staring at on a sheet of paper to the three-dimensional world that is unfolded in front of you.

Aside from the obvious roads, trails, rivers, and streams, the most useful information on your map is contained in the contours. A contour line is a line that denotes a certain elevation on the map, and the contour interval is the amount of vertical distance between each line. If you remember nothing else about this part of the book remember this: close contour lines = steep, and wide contour lines = sloping.

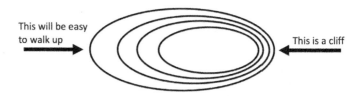

This will be easy to walk up

This is a cliff

If this seems downright obvious, consider that hundreds of TBS students each year seem to miss this concept altogether and lead their classmates on painfully unnecessary mountaineering trips that could be avoided by some simple examination of the contour lines.

From some basic reading of the terrain on the map you can also determine your location. If you are near a bend in the river, where is that on the map? Where do the contour lines match the hills and valleys that are standing in front of you? Don't just read the map—*read the terrain.* Once you have a decent understanding of where you are and where you are going, the next step is figuring out the direction you need to walk.

The essential tool for determining direction is a compass. A compass is a simple navigation tool consisting of a container, which holds a magnetized needle that points to earth's magnetic north pole (not to be confused with the *geographic* north pole, the axis upon which the earth rotates and where all lines of longitude converge). In our modern day and age, even most smartphones have some sort of compass function built into them.

---

**Direction can also be roughly determined by the position of the sun based on time of day (rises in the east, sets in the west). Another less common method used in any kind of urban terrain is to look at satellite dishes—since most communications satellites sit in geostationary orbit above the equator, if you are in the northern hemisphere, dishes will point *generally* south (the opposite is true in the southern hemisphere).**

---

Next time you are out in the wilderness, try to pay attention to which direction you are moving. Tie in your direction of movement with your reading of the terrain. Which direction does the terrain slope? Does a trail run generally north-south? East-west? The earth rarely conveniences you with terrain that holds one specific direction, and understanding the direction you are facing at any given time will inform the path you take.

Rounding out the holy trinity of navigation is the distance you must travel from origin to destination. Given nothing other than a destination and a direction, how will you know when you will reach it? Distance can inform quite a bit about what the military refers to as "time-space logistics." How long will it take you to hike one mile? Two miles? Three? What does that tell you about your food and water supply? If an emergency happens, what is the distance and direction to the nearest source of help?

Distance while hiking is relatively easy to measure but requires nuance to understand. A good measurement is a "pace count." Pace counts are easy to figure out and tailored to each individual. One pace is one step with *each foot*—that is, left, right, one... left, right, two... and so on. The standard method for determining your pace count is to walk two hundred meters (the military does everything in the metric system, but this works just as easily done in yards), while counting your total number of paces, then divide that number by two. The number you are left with is the best-estimate number of paces you will take to cover one hundred meters.

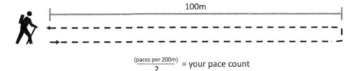

$$\frac{(\text{paces per 200m})}{2} = \text{your pace count}$$

The nuance of your pace count comes when you begin to factor in everything else we have discussed. What type of terrain are you walking up? Steep grades will shorten your steps, increasing your pace count. Carrying a heavy load on your back will do the same. Running will lengthen your stride and decrease your pace count. As you traverse various terrain your pace count will change, which is something to regularly monitor. Pace count beads (detailed in the *Navigation* chapter of this book) are an invaluable tool. The pace count beads I used for a good portion of my military career were ones I fashioned out of zip ties tightly-wrapped around lengths of nylon parachute cord. Given nothing else, put a rock in your pocket every hundred meters to keep track of long distances.

The average hiker today will have an abundance of technological resources for quickly determining location, direction, and distance. Indeed, even military forces today have largely evolved beyond manual navigation on the battlefield, instead using satellites to determine mensurated grid locations down to the meter. In spite of all of the marvels of technology, basic map-and-compass land navigation is the hallmark of many special operations selection and training programs. Why? Because the confidence that comes with mastery of terrain and respect for the earth's phlegmatic indifference to the human condition is preconditional to standing tall in front of others and saying, "Follow me."

# APPENDIX B:
# PROFESSION

―――

*"Down here in the dirt there are no politics."*
—JUSTIN EGGEN, "NO POLITICS," IN LOVE…&WAR

For a long time, I thought about the stark dichotomy created when less-than-just killing occurs in war. Ostensibly, we go forth into the breach for god and country, to protect the people and way of life we hold so dearly. The truth of the matter is a significant portion of us raise our hand and pick up a gun for less honorable reasons. Karl Marlantes puts it bluntly in his hard-hitting book *What It Is Like to Go to War*: "Combat is the crack cocaine of all excitement highs– with crack cocaine costs."[161] So many people who set foot onto the yellow footprints at Parris Island, South Carolina, or San

―――

161 Marlantes, a Rhodes Scholar at Oxford University, also relates a story of how he met Joseph Campbell in a hotel bar, where the two proceeded to have a long conversation over dinner and whiskey discussing killing, intension, and absolution. Karl Marlantes, *What It Is Like to Go to War*, (New York: Atlantic Monthly Press, 2011), 160.

Diego, California, are lusting after the sense of belonging that comes when you pray at the temple of Mars, the god of war.[162]

"Killing in war isn't always the morally clean 'it was them or me' situation which we so often hear about," Marlantes explains. "The more technically sophisticated we get, in fact, the less common this situation will become, and the more problematic the morality."[163] This became especially true in the Global War on Terror. In February 2001, an experimental version of the MQ-1 "Predator" Remotely Piloted Aircraft (i.e., drone) successfully fired three Hellfire missiles into a target in the deserts of Nevada, just a short drive from Las Vegas. The Central Intelligence Agency and Department of Defense had spent the previous year flying unarmed Predators over Afghanistan, trying to pinpoint Osama Bin Laden.

The ability to arm RPAs represents a monumental shift in how killing in war occurs, allowing missions to be flown all over the world, piloted from an air-conditioned office building with a taco truck parked outside and a Starbucks on the corner. This is an evolution of what David Grossman refers to as the "mechanical distance" of killing—referring to the dampening of the psychological effects of killing the further we get away from it.[164] Just a few steps further and we are Ender Wiggin, playing Orson Scott Card's sci-fi simulation, unwittingly ordering the deaths of thousands with the flick of a joystick and the push of a button.[165]

---

162  The location of the Marine Corps' two recruit training depots.
163  Karl Marlantes, *What It Is Like to Go to War*, 36.
164  Dave Grossman, *On Killing*, (New York: Back Bay Books, 2009), 108-109.
165  Orson Scott Card, *Ender's Game*, (New York: Tor Books, 1985).

Despite the technological advancements that have allowed us to find, fix, and finish our enemies with extraordinary efficiency, at the end of the day, sometimes we get it wrong. Here lies the dichotomy: being a consummately professional killer and sometimes just getting it plain wrong. In the confusion of the night the wrong house is targeted, an individual is misidentified, and deadly consequences play out in real time, like a locomotive running full speed off the track.

After I returned from Afghanistan I gave a lecture to a group of law students describing my experience dealing with both Afghan Rule of Law and the internationally agreed upon Laws of Armed Conflict. In my experience, the simple fact of the matter is that most of the time in war, there is no procedural due process. There is no appealing a sentence once it exits the barrel of a rifle at 2,500 feet per second. This is not an apologist plea to say that in many cases we could not have done better. Rather, the observation I took away was merely that many Marines pride themselves in doing a good job—and sometimes the job that is done turns out to be a result of faulty logic all the way from the top down.

I tried unsuccessfully for several years to capture these thoughts in a work of short fiction. However, in 2018, as I floated lazily down the Mekong River through Laos, devoid of any connection with the outside world, I decided to change my medium, capturing the imagery I had carried in my head in a few short verses. The poem that resulted was printed in Dead Reckoning Collective's anthology *In Love...&War* and is reprinted below.

**Wicked Profession**
Gear check, comm check, press check
Eyes, lights, sights
Pre-dawn insert
In'jin country
Silent nighttime trek

Past the river
Down the wadi
Green cratered moonscape
Single file down
Empty alleys
Through the compound gate

Build the hide site
Frigid cold
Long guns on the roof
Poncho liners
Piss in bottles
Muddy frozen boots

Sun is rising
Crack door open
Peek over the wall
Bazaar filling
Up with people
Prayers are being call'd

Signal picked up
Target moving
Slew drone sensors west
Triangulate

Disseminate
Alert the QRF

Light brown man dress
Jet black turban
'cross the wadi now
Talk the hogs on
Twist the turrets
Crosshairs on his brow

On the bridge
It's now or never
Pull the slack out slow
First round rings out
Sky rips open
Three more fast in tow

Judges, jurors
Execution'rs
Death by firing squad
Head split open
Brains are scattered
Sent off to his god

Throw our plates on
Sprint to kill zone
Cordon off far side
Search the body
Transmit pictures
Shit, this ain't our guy

Crowd is gath'ring

Break down hide site
Trucks are round the bend
Move to extract
Home by lunchtime
Warm and safe again

Mission debrief
Intel updates
Target still alive
Lucky bastard
Back to planning
We'll get him next time

In the street
A fam'ly mourning
Borne into this hell
But can we feel bad
That we can kill so well?

# ACKNOWLEDGEMENTS

————

The epigraph of *A narrative life of David Crockett, written by himself,* reads:

I leave this rule for others when I'm dead,
Be always sure you're right—THEN
GO AHEAD!

I rarely undertake an endeavor that I am not willing to see through to its bitter end. So, when Eric Koester reached out to me about writing a book, I approached the opportunity with my usual skepticism. I sought the opinions of peers I respected who had published with New Degree Press, and ultimately decided that I would write The Lonesome Thread, if for no reason other than just for the sake of writing it. To those individuals I sought out for counsel early on in the formation of this book—thank you for pointing me down this path.

A big thank you to the individuals who donated their time, stories, and thoughts which went on to become the foundation for this book. Particularly Keith Dow, Tyler Carroll, Becca Shopiro, Lisa Directo-Davis, and Julia Bainbridge.

Thank you to my editors, Michael Bailey and Morgan Rohde, who kept me on task and ensured that this book came out as a complete thought. And thank you to the Eric Koester and the entire New Degree Press team who played a part in producing this book: Mateusz Cichosz, Gjorgji Pejkovski, Venus Bradley, Amanda Brown, and Brian Bies.

Thanks as well to all of the wonderful people who pre-ordered the copies of the book. Pre-orders are important to authors, and they made publishing The Lonesome Thread possible. Despite writing a book about solitude, I was overwhelmed by the amount of support and encouragement I received from countless terrific people around the country and around the world. Those of you who reached out to give early feedback on the manuscript were an integral part to an extensive revisions process.

Shout out to everyone who helped promote The Lonesome Thread through word of mouth, and a special thanks to Mackenzie Wolf and Prashant Malaviya for putting this book in the spotlight and spreading the word through the veteran and Georgetown communities.

My eternal gratitude to the following readers:

Feysel Abdulkaf*
Adam Aikens
Esperanza Alzona*
Eduardo Alzona*
Estevan Astorga
Maria Ayers
Ryan Beasley
Dani Bernstein
Galo Bowen
Gordon Bradshaw
Christopher Brahm
Christopher Brill
Dan Brown
Johnathan Brown*
Emma Byer
Caitlin Callahan
Ali Carpenter
Alli Cavasino
Daniel Corcoran
Dena Crosson
Neal Crosson
Jean Crosson & Chris Sealy*
Tommy Crosson
Stephen Czarkowski
Rohan Dalvi
Lisa Da Silva
Loren Dauberman
Ben Davis
Michael DeMarseilles
Nicholas Folts
Andrew Fredell
Anne Fredell*

John and Diane Fredell*
Maria Giovanna Galasso
McKinley Gillespie
Andy Gordon
Annika Grangaard
Anthony Grzincic
Adam Gutman
Michael Hagan
Nicholas Hann
Chris Howell
Philip Hussey
Jessica Junker
Chong Kim
Benjamin King
Jacques Klick
Eric Koester
Kyle MacKinnon
Prashant Malaviya
Doug McCausland
Kevin McNamee
Lawrence Montreuil
Robert Musso
Eduardo Ocampo
James and Alexis Pollock*
Alex Poulin
Varun Premkumar
Lisa Putnam
Steph Puzak
Mackenzie Rae
Vail Raymer
Taylor Reeves
Chris Rose

# WORKS CITED

——

**INTRODUCTION**

Beer, Chris. "Is TikTok Setting the Scene for Music on Social Media?" GlobalWebIndex, January 3, 2019. https://blog.global-webindex.com/trends/tiktok-music-social-media.

DataReportal. "Global Social Media Overview." Accessed August 24, 2020. https://datareportal.com/social-media-users.

LinkedIn. "LinkedIn Statistics Page." accessed August 24, 2020. https://news.linkedin.com/about-us#Statistics.

Lin, Ying. "10 Twitter Statistics Every Marketer Should Know in 2020." Oberlo, May 30, 2020. https://www.oberlo.com/blog/twitter-statistics.

Omnicore. "Instagram by the Numbers: Stats, Demographics & Fun Facts." Accessed August 24, 2020. https://www.omnicore-agency.com/instagram-statistics.

Statista. "Daily time spent with the internet per capita worldwide from 2011 to 2021, by device." Accessed August 24, 2020. https://www.statista.com/statistics/319732/daily-time-spent-online-device.

Statista. "Number of monthly active Facebook users worldwide as of 2nd quarter 2020." Accessed August 24, 2020. https://www.statista.com/statistics/264810/number-of-monthly-active-facebook-users-worldwide.

## TIME & SPACE

**RETREAT**

Ahmed, Will. "Andy Puddicombe, Buddhist Monk and Co-Founder of Headspace." February 27, 2019, In WHOOP Podcast. Podcast, MP3 audio, 1:29:22. https://www.whoop.com/thelocker/podcast-12-andy-puddicombe-buddhist-monk-headspace-co-founder/.

Barol, Bill. "The Monk And The Mad Man Making Mindfulness For The Masses." Fast Company, January 28, 2015. https://www.fastcompany.com/3041402/the-monk-and-the-mad-man-making-mindfulness-for-the-masses.

Beach Tomato. "Get Some Headspace: Q&A with Andy Puddicombe." Accessed August 24, 2020. https://www.beachtomato.com/lifestyle/get-some-headspace-qa-with-andy-puddicombe.

Camus, Albert. The Myth of Sisyphus and Other Essays. Translated by Justin O'Brien. New York: Random House LLC, 2012.

Chaykowski, Kathleen. "Meet Headspace, The App That Made Meditation A $250 Million Business." Forbes, January 8, 2017. https://www.forbes.com/sites/kathleenchaykowski/2017/01/08/meet-headspace-the-app-that-made-meditation-a-250-million-business.

Connett, David. "Second victim in Christmas crash." The Independent, December 27, 1992. https://www.independent.co.uk/news/uk/second-victim-in-christmas-crash-1565578.html.

Goode, Lauren and Kara Swisher. "Headspace meditation app co-founder and CEO Rich Pierson." July 7, 2017, In Too Embarrassed to Ask. Produced by Vox Media. Podcast, MP3 audio, 47:08. https://www.vox.com/2017/7/7/15931118/transcript-headspace-meditation-app-co-founder-ceo-rich-pierson-too-embarrassed-to-ask.

The Guardian. "BP in Russia: a timeline." October 18, 2012. Accessed August 24, 2020. https://www.theguardian.com/business/2012/oct/18/bp-russia-history-timeline-rosneft.

P Funk. "Declutter your mind on the Central Line." Evening Standard, April 14, 2010. https://www.standard.co.uk/lifestyle/health/declutter-your-mind-on-the-central-line-6458946.html.

Powell-Smith, Anna. "Keynsham." Open Domesday. Accessed October 7, 2020. https://opendomesday.org/place/ST6568/keynsham/.

Puddicombe, Andy. The Headspace Guide to Meditation and Mindfulness: How Mindfulness Can Change Your Life in Ten Minutes a Day. New York: St. Martin's Publishing Group, 2012.

Puddicombe, Andy. "Why 10 Minutes Each Day Can Change Your Day," Produced by DO Wales, DO. 2012, Video, 20:17. https://vimeo.com/58869661.

Jacqueline, Rachel. "Headspace app co-founder and monk Andy Puddicombe talks mindfulness," Post Magazine, May 30, 2015. https://www.scmp.com/magazines/post-magazine/article/1811119/headspace-app-co-founder-and-monk-andy-puddicombe-talks.

Jenkin, Matthew. "Mind over cancer: can meditation aid recovery?" The Guardian, February 14, 2020. https://www.theguardian.com/society/2014/feb/14/cancer-meditation-aid-recovery.

Rose, Ted. "The Power of Solitude." Tricycle, Spring 2005. https://tricycle.org/magazine/power-solitude.

Sehmi, Sunita. "Meditation isn't about eliminating stress from your life it's about learning to sit with it. Andy Puddicombe invites us all to get some Headspace." Thrive Global, May 20, 2019. https://thriveglobal.com/stories/meditation-isnt-about-eliminating-stress-from-your-life-its-about-learning-to-sit-with-it-andy-puddicombe-invites-us-all-to-get-some-headspace.

Shieber, Jonathan. "Headspace raises $93 Million in equity and debt as it pursues clinical validation for mindfulness." Tech Crunch, February 12, 2020. https://techcrunch.com/2020/02/12/headspace-raises-53-million-and-40-million-in-debt-as-it-pursues-clinical-validation-for-mindfulness.

Silverberg, David. "Scaling mindfulness: How the Headspace cofounders used the NBA, Delta Airlines, and The Guardian

newspaper to bring meditation to 60 million users." Business
Insider, November 29, 2019. https://www.businessinsider.com/
headspace-cofounders-nba-delta-the-guardian-brought-med-
itation-million-users.

Widdicombe, Lizzie. "The Higher Life." The New Yorker, June 29,
2015. https://www.newyorker.com/magazine/2015/07/06/the-
higher-life.


**RETROGRADE**

Appleman, Roy. Escaping the Trap: The US Army X Corps in
Northeast Korea, 1950. College Station, Texas: Texas A&M
University, 1990.

Bevin, Alexander. Korea: The First War We Lost. New York: Hippocrene Books, 1986.

Commandership at the Chosin Reservoir: A Triumph of Optimism
and Resilience. Quantico, VA: Marine Corps University, 2019.

Field Manual 100-15: Corps Operations. Washington, DC: Department of the Army, 1996.

Hughes, John C. Jim Evans. Olympia, Washington: Legacy Washington, 2017. https://www.sos.wa.gov/_assets/legacy/jim-evans.
pdf.

Janssen, Volker. "The Most Harrowing Battle of the Korean War."
History. Accessed August 25, 2020. https://www.history.com/
news/korean-war-chosin-reservoir-veterans-stories.

MacArthur, Douglas. "Home by Christmas." November 28, 1950. https://www.trumanlibrary.gov/public/MacArthur_DocumentSet.

MacLowry, Randall, dir. American Experience, season 28, episode 8, "The Battle of Chosin." Aired November 1, 2016, on PBS.

Mossman, Billy C. Ebb and Flow: November 1950-July 1951. Washington, DC: U.S. Government Printing Office, 1990. https://history.army.mil/html/books/020/20-4/index.html.

Natanson, Elad. "Healthcare Apps: A Boon, Today And Tomorrow." Forbes, July 21, 2020. https://www.forbes.com/sites/eladnatanson/2020/07/21/healthcare-apps-a-boon-today-and-tomorrow.

Walters, Mary Lou. "Hero Of The Chosin Reservoir." The Eastwick Press, April 11, 2014. https://eastwickpress.com/news/2014/04/hero-of-the-chosin-reservoir.

## ISOLATION

de Botton, Alain. The Consolations of Philosophy. New York: Vintage Books, 2000.

Collins, Jim. Good to Great. New York: Harper Business, 2001.

Lange, Kate. "Medal of Honor Monday: Navy Vice Adm. James Stockdale." DoD News, March 2, 2020. https://www.defense.gov/Explore/Features/story/Article/2097870/medal-of-honor-monday-navy-vice-adm-james-stockdale.

The National Aviation Hall of Fame. "Stockdale, James Bond." Accessed August 25, 2020. https://www.nationalaviation.org/our-enshrinees/stockdale-james-bond.

Stockdale, James. Courage Under Fire: Testing Epictetus's Doctrines in a Laboratory of Human Behavior. Stanford, CA: Hoover Institution Press, 1993.


## DEFEAT

Ayahuasca.com (blog). "Ayahuasca, Religion and Nature." March 27, 2008. Accessed August 27, 2020. http://www.ayahuasca.com/introductions/ayahuasca-religion-and-nature.

Brodrick, James. Saint Ignatius Loyola: The Pilgrim Years 1491-1538. San Francisco, California: Ignatius Press, 1998.

Montserrat Tourist Guide. "Black Madonna at Montserrat: The Image of the Virgin Mary." Accessed October 7, 2020. https://www.montserrat-tourist-guide.com/en/attractions/black-madonna-montserrat-spain.html.

Saint Ignatius of Loyola. A Pilgrim's Journey: The Autobiography of Ignatius of Loyola, translated by Joseph N. Tylenda S.J. San Francisco, California: Ignatius Press, 2017.

Saint Ignatius of Loyola. The Life of St. Ignatius of Loyola, Founder of the Jesuits, ed. F. Francesco Mariani. London: Thomas Richardson and Son, 1847.

Seneca, Lucius Annaeus. Letters from a Stoic. translated by Robin Campbell. London: Penguin Books, 1969.

# TOOLS & REFLECTIONS

## PRESENCE

Germain, Brian. Green Light Your Life: Awakening Your Higher Self. Rockville, Maryland: Adventure Wisdom LLC, 2013.

Germain, Brian. Transcending Fear: The Doorway to Freedom. Rockville, Maryland: Adventure Wisdom LLC, 2013.

Kaufman, Scott Barry. "The Creative 'Flow': How to Enter That Mysterious State of Oneness." HuffPost, January 25, 2012. https://www.huffpost.com/entry/consciousness-and-flow_b_1108113.

Petranker, Jack. "The Present Moment." Tricycle (blog). Winter 2014. Accessed August 27, 2020. https://tricycle.org/magazine/present-moment.

Rohr, Richard. Falling Upward: A Spirituality for the Two Halves of Life. San Francisco, California: Jossey-Bass, 2011.

Sheldon, Kennon M., Mike Prentice, and Marc Halusic, "The Experiential Incompatibility of Mindfulness and Flow Absorption," Social Psychological and Personality Science, vol. 6, 3, (November, 2015): 276-283. https://doi.org/10.1177/2F1948550614555028.

Skydive Orange (blog). "The Art of Keeping Calm." January 30, 2020. Accessed August 27, 2020. https://www.skydiveorange.com/2020/01/30/the-art-of-keeping-calm.

TED. "How craving attention makes you less creative | Joseph Gordon-Levitt." Uploaded 12 September 2019. YouTube video, 13:15. https://youtu.be/3VTsIju1dLI.

TEDx. "Extreme Ownership | Jocko Willink | TEDxUniversity-ofNevada." Uploaded 2 February 2017. YouTube video, 13:49. https://youtu.be/ljqra3BcqWM.

United States Parachute Association. "Skydiving Safety." Accessed August 27, 2020. https://uspa.org/find/faqs/safety.


**BOREDOM**

American Psychological Association. "Multitasking: Switching costs." March 20, 2006. Accessed August 29, 2020. https://www.apa.org/research/action/multitask.

Bainbridge, Julia. "Inner Lives: Why Boredom Leads to Creativity, with Manoush Zomorodi." July, 2019. In The Lonely Hour. Produced by Julia Bainbridge. Podcast, MP3 audio, 9:29. https://www.thelonelyhour.com/episodes#/manoush-zomorodi.

Bank of America. "Trends in Consumer Mobility Report 2015." 2015. Accessed August 29, 2020. https://www.slideshare.net/Phildu1/bank-of-america-2015-consumer-mobility-report.

Banks, Siobhan, Jillian Dorrian, and Cassie J. Hilditch. "Time to wake up: reactive countermeasures to sleep inertia." Industrial Health, 54 (November 2016), 528-541. https://dx.doi.org/10.2486%2Findhealth.2015-0236.

Brownlee, Dana. "This Dangerous Morning Habit May Sabotage Your Productivity All Day." Forbes. September 10, 2020. https://www.forbes.com/sites/danabrownlee/2020/09/10/this-dangerous-morning-habit-may-sabotage-your-productivity-all-day.

Centers for Disease Control and Prevention. "Data and Statistics About ADHD." October 15, 2019. Accessed August 29, 2020. https://www.cdc.gov/ncbddd/adhd/data.html.

Cohen, Rony, Batia Cohen-Kroitoru, Ayelet Halevy, Sharon Aharoni, Irena Aizenberg, and Avinoam Shuper. "Handwriting in children with Attention Deficient Hyperactive Disorder: role of graphology." BMC Pediatrics, 19 (December 10, 2019): 484. https://dx.doi.org/10.1186%2Fs12887-019-1854-3.

Cramer-Flood, Ethan. "Global Digital Ad Spending Update Q2 2020." eMarketer, July 6, 2020. Accessed August 29, 2020. https://www.emarketer.com/content/global-digital-ad-spending-update-q2-2020.

DataReportal. "Digital 2020: April Global Statshot." April, 2020. Accessed August 29, 2020. https://datareportal.com/reports/digital-2020-april-global-statshot.

Enhanced Performance Systems. "The Attentional & Interpersonal Style Inventory: Business Report Sample." Accessed August 29, 2020. https://epstais.com/rpts.cgi?k=elA54nyuvUppBykm&v.

Ferriss, Timothy. "Relax Like A Pro: 5 Steps to Hacking Your Sleep." The Tim Ferriss Show (blog). January 27, 2008. Accessed August 29, 2020. https://tim.blog/2008/01/27/relax-like-a-pro-5-steps-to-hacking-your-sleep.

Harari, Yuval Noah. Homo Deus. Trans. by the author. New York: HarperCollins Publishers, 2017.

IDC. "Always Connected: How Smartphones and Social Keep Us Engaged." 2013. Accessed June 20, 2020. https://www.nu.nl/files/IDC-Facebook%20Always%20Connected%20(1).pdf.

Jones, Chuck, Abe Levitow, and Dave Monahan, dirs. The Phantom Tollbooth. VHS. Culver City, California: MGM Animation/Visual Arts, 1970.

Konnikova, Maria. "Multitask Masters." The New Yorker, May 7, 2014. https://www.newyorker.com/science/maria-konnikova/multitask-masters.

Murnane, Elizabeth L., Saeed Abdullah, Mark Matthews, Matthew Kay, Julie A. Kientz, Tanzeem Choudhury, Geri Gay, and Dan Cosley. "Mobile Manifestations of Alertness: Connecting Biological Rhythms with Patterns of Smartphone App Use." MobileHCI, 16 (September 2016), 465-477. https://pac.cs.cornell.edu/pubs/MobileHCI2016_MobileManifesations.pdf.

National Institute of Mental Health. "Attention-Deficit/Hyperactivity Disorder (ADHD)." November, 2017. Accessed August 29, 2020. https://www.nimh.nih.gov/health/statistics/attention-deficit-hyperactivity-disorder-adhd.shtml.

Nideffer, Robert M. "Reliability and Validity of The Attentional and Interpersonal Style (TAIS) Inventory Concentration Scales." In D. Smith & M. Bar-Eli (Eds.). Essential readings in sport and exercise psychology (pp. 265-277). Champaign, IL: Human Kinetics. https://api.semanticscholar.org/CorpusID:30271905.

Sweitzer, Letitia. The Elephant in the ADHD Room: Beating Boredom as the Secret to Managing ADHD. London: Jessica Kingsley Publishers, 2014.

Swisher, Kara and Scott Galloway. "Tesla's "Battery Day", the DOJ prepares for Google, and Scott's prediction on "algorithmic e-commerce," 25 September, 2020, in Pivot, produced by Vox Media, podcast, MP3 audio, 1:03:25. https://megaphone.link/VMP9418534948.

TED. "How boredom can lead to your most brilliant ideas | Manoush Zomorodi." Uploaded 29 August 2017. YouTube video, 16:13. https://youtu.be/c73Q80Qmwzo.

Uriarte, Maximilian. "Terminal Lance #41 "Standing Post: Stages of Boredom." Terminal Lance (blog). June 8, 2010. Accessed August 28, 2020. https://terminallance.com/2010/06/08/terminal-lance-41-standing-post-stages-of-boredom.

Wilson, Timothy D., David A. Reinhard, Erin C. Westgate, Daniel T. Gilbert, Nicole Ellerbeck, Cheryl Hahn, Casey L. Brown, Adi Shaked. "Just think: The challenges of the disengaged mind." Science, 345 (July 2014): 75-77. https://doi.org/ 10.1126/science.1250830.

**ANALOG**

Basford, Johanna. "Johanna Basford," Johanna Basford's Personal Website. https://www.johannabasford.com.

Grossoman, Dave. On Killing. New York: Back Bay Books, 2009.

VanRy, Nikki. "What Happened to Adult Coloring Books? Charting the Boom and Bust," Book Riot. November 6, 2019. https://bookriot.com/adult-coloring-books-trend.

Zomorodi, Manoush. Bored and Brilliant: How Spacing Out Can Unlock Your Most Productive and Creative Self. New York: St. Martin's Press, 2017.

**STRUCTURE**

Albanese, Alexa. "Tim Ferriss: How to Rig the Game So You Can Win It." Creative Live. December 9, 2016. https://www.creativelive.com/blog/tim-ferriss-success-habits.

Cao, Jerry, Kamil Zieba and Matt Ellis. "Why White Space Is Crucial To UX Design." Fast Company. May 28, 2015. Accessed 11 September 2020. https://www.fastcompany.com/3046656/why-white-space-is-crucial-to-ux-design.

Ferriss, Timothy. The 4-Hour Chef: The Simple Path to Cooking Like a Pro, Learning Anything, and Living The Good Life. New York: Houghton Mifflin Harcourt Publishing Company, 2012.

Matthews, Gail. "Goals Research Summary." July 23, 2007. https://scholar.dominican.edu/cgi/viewcontent.cgi?article=1265&context=news-releases.

Mind Tools (blog). "Smart Goals: How to Make Your Goals Achievable." Accessed 11 September 2020. https://www.mindtools.com/pages/article/smart-goals.htm.

P.O.W. Network. "Bio, Stavast, John E." Accessed 13 September 2020. https://www.pownetwork.org/bios/s/s064.htm.

Sutherland, Jeff and J.J. Sutherland. Scrum: The Art of Doing Twice the Work in Half the Time. New York: Currency, 2014.

Sweitzer, Letitia. The Elephant in the ADHD Room: Beating Boredom as the Secret to Managing ADHD. London: Jessica Kingsley Publishers, 2014.

Weller, Craig. "The Three Rs," Hitter Feed (blog), OAF Nation, August 6, 2020, accessed 22 September 2020. http://oafnation.com/the-three-rs.

Withers, Douglas. "Air Force 432nd Tactical Reconnaissance Wing." Together We Served. Accessed 13 September 2020. https://airforce.togetherweserved.com/usaf/servlet/tws.webapp.WebApp?cmd=PublicUnitProfile&type=Unit&ID=9570.

## CREATION & GRATITUDE

### PERFORMANCE

Arceneaux, Kevin. "Anxiety Reduces Empathy Toward Outgroup Members But Not Ingroup Members," Journal of Experimental Political Science, 4, no. 1, (Spring 2017): 68-80. https://doi.org/10.1017/XPS.2017.12.

Frimmel, Kayla. "Mental Preparation Techniques and Accomplishments of Race Goals by Ironman Triathletes: A Qualitative Investigation" (master's thesis, Georgia Southern University,

2012). https://digitalcommons.georgiasouthern.edu/cgi/view-content.cgi?article=1128&context=etd.

Georgetown Law. "The Center on Poverty and Inequality." Accessed September 16, 2020. https://www.law.georgetown.edu/poverty-inequality-center.

Guszkowska, Monika. "Effects of exercise on anxiety, depression and mood [in Polish]." Psychiatria Polska, 38 (2004): 611–620. https://pubmed.ncbi.nlm.nih.gov/15518309/.

Plante, Thomas. "Your Exercise Environment Matters a Lot." Psychology Today (blog). February 10, 2015. https://www.psychologytoday.com/us/blog/do-the-right-thing/201502/your-exercise-environment-matters-lot.

Sharma, Ashish, Vishal Madaan, and Frederick D. Petty, "Exercise for Mental Health." The Primary Care Companion to the Journal of Clinical Psychiatry, 8, no. 2 (2006): 106. https://dx.doi.org/10.4088%2Fpcc.v08n0208a.

Spreng, R. Nathan, Kathy D. Gerlach, Gary R. Turner, Daniel L. Schacter. "Autobiographical planning and the brain: Activation and its modulation by qualitative features," Journal of Cognitive Neuroscience, 27, no. 11 (2015): 2147-57. https://doi.org/10.1162/jocn_a_00846.

TED. "How boredom can lead to your most brilliant ideas | Manoush Zomorodi." Uploaded 29 August 2017. YouTube video, 16:13. https://youtu.be/c73Q8oQmwzo.

**COLLECTIVE**

Cooper, Tim. "A Fresh Voice in the Veteran Community? Meet Dead Reckoning Collective." Coffee or Die Magazine. May 6, 2019. https://coffeeordie.com/dead-reckoning-collective.

Gerino, Eva, Luca Rollè, Cristina Sechi, and Piera Brustia. "Loneliness, Resilience, Mental Health, and Quality of Life in Old Age: A Structural Equation Model." Frontiers in Psychology, no. 8 (November 2017): 2003. https://dx.doi.org/10.3389%2Ffpsyg.2017.02003.

Harris, Kent. "Four soldiers honored at Vicenza memorial service." Stars and Stripes. August 2, 2012. https://www.stripes.com/news/europe/four-soldiers-honored-at-vicenza-memorial-service-1.184702.


**MONOMYTH**

Campbell, Joseph. The Hero with a Thousand Faces. California: New World Library, 2008.

Doré, Bruce P. "Helping Others Regulate Emotion Predicts Increased Regulation of One's Own Emotions and Decreased Symptoms of Depression." Personality and Social Psychology Bulletin. 43, no. 5 (2017): 729-739. https://doi.org/10.1177%2F0146167217695558.

Esalen. "Joseph Campbell." Accessed 14 September 2020. https://www.esalen.org/page/joseph-campbell.

Galloway, Scott. The Algebra of Happiness: Notes on the Pursuit of Success, Love, and Meaning, New York: Portfolio, 2019.

Printed in Great Britain
by Amazon

20170964R00129

Helliwell, John, Richard Layard, and Jeffrey Sachs. "World Happiness Report." The Earth Institute. Commissioned for the United Nations Conference on Happiness. New York, NY, April 2, 2012). https://issuu.com/earthinstitute/docs/world-happiness-report.

Pacific Graduate Institute Alumni Association (blog). "Joseph Campbell Gets a Tree in Carmel-by-the-Sea." May 2, 2018. Accessed 14 September 2020. https://pgiaa.org/news-announcements/joseph-campbell-gets-a-tree-in-carmel-by-the-sea.

Post, Steven G. "Altruism, happiness, and health: it's good to be good." International Journal of Behavioral Medicine. 12, (2005): 66-77. https://greatergood.berkeley.edu/images/uploads/Post-AltruismHappinessHealth.pdf.

Rohr, Richard. Falling Upward: A Spirituality for the Two Halves of Life. San Francisco: Jossey-Bass, 2011.

Rohr, Richard. "The Two Halves of Life." Daily Meditations (blog). Center for Action and Contemplation. October 12, 2015. https://cac.org/two-halves-life-2015-10-12.

Seastrom, Lucas. "Mythic Discovery Within the Inner Reaches of Outer Space: Joseph Campbell Meets George Lucas - Part I." October 22, 2015. Accessed 14 September 2020. https://www.starwars.com/news/mythic-discovery-within-the-inner-reaches-of-outer-space-joseph-campbell-meets-george-lucas-part-i.

**APPENDIX B: PROFESSION**
Card, Orson Scott. Ender's Game. New York: Tor Books, 1985.

Grossman, Dave. On Killing. New York: Back Bay Books, 2009.

Marlantes, Karl. What It Is Like to Go to War. New York: Atlantic Monthly Press, 2011.